B+T
2/96

J970.2W

We Rode the Wind

Recollections of Native American Life

Compiled and Edited by Jane B. Katz

RP

RUNESTONE PRESS

Minneapolis, Minnesota

RUNESTONE PRESS • RUNESTONE

rune (roon) *n* **1 a :** one of the earliest written alphabets used in northern Europe, dating back to A.D. 200; **b :** an alphabet character believed to have magic powers; **c :** a charm; **d :** an Old Norse or Finnish poem. **2 :** a poem or incantation of mysterious significance, often carved in stone.

We Rode the Wind: Recollections of Native American Life is a fully revised and updated edition of *We Rode the Wind: Recollections of Nineteenth-Century Tribal Life*, a title previously published by Lerner Publications Company. The text is completely reset in 12/14 Goudy, and new photographs and captions have been added.

The sources for all the selections used in this anthology are listed in the back of the book, beginning on page 125. Every effort has been made to contact the copyright holders of the material quoted in this book, and grateful acknowledgment is made to all those who gave permission to reprint passages from their works. Any omissions that are brought to our attention will be acknowledged and credited in subsequent printings of this book.

Words in **bold** type are listed in a glossary that begins on page 122.

Library of Congress Cataloging-in-Publication Data

We rode the wind: recollections of Native American life / compiled and edited by Jane B. Katz.
   p. cm.
   Includes Index.
   ISBN 0-8225-3154-2 (lib. bdg.)
   1. Indians of North America—Juvenile literature. 2. Indians of North American—Biography—Juvenile literature. [1. Indians of North America. 2. Indians of North America—Biography.] I. Katz, Jane B.
E77.4.W38 1995
978'.00497'00922'—dc20
[B]   94-34946
                                                                       CIP
                                                                        AC

Manufactured in the United States of America
1 2 3 4 5 6 - JR - 00 99 98 97 96 95

Contents

Preface

The Plains Indians were important historians of nineteenth-century life on the Great Plains, a region including what are now the states of Montana, Wyoming, North Dakota, South Dakota, Minnesota, Iowa, Nebraska, Colorado, Kansas, Missouri, Oklahoma, New Mexico, Arkansas, and Texas. Their memoirs reveal keen observations of Native American life and the changing world in which they lived. As narrators of their people's past, these historians were knowledgeable, perceptive, and honest.

But many of the writers spoke only their native language and had to rely on translators to put their ideas into English. For the most part, these translators were skillful and sincere. Yet Indian languages are diverse and complex. Sometimes translators had difficulty finding the exact wordings. Furthermore, most of the interpreters were white and tended to change the writings to make them more appealing to white readers. Thus, as with any translation, some of the flavor and spontaneity of the original Indian works were lost.

In putting together this collection, I have been careful to select material that, to the best of my knowledge, is faithful to the intent, the spirit, and the wording of the Indian authors.

Jane B. Katz

A group of Sioux (also called Dakota or Lakota) set up their camp along a riverbank in South Dakota in the late 1800s.

Introduction

In the nineteenth century, many Indian groups inhabited the Great Plains. This vast, windswept area of North America extended westward from the Mississippi River to the Rocky Mountains and northward from Texas to southern Canada. Some Indian peoples had been living on the Plains since prehistoric times. Other groups migrated there much later from the Eastern Woodlands, an area that covered the eastern third of the United States. Over the centuries, the eastern Indians adopted the lifestyles of their neighbors on the Plains.

The Plains Indians, like other Indian groups in North America, were organized into political units called nations, or tribes. Each tribe had its own distinct history and customs. Sometimes nations were divided further into smaller groups called bands. Each band, for example, may have lived in a different village within the tribe's territory.

Geographical factors largely determined a group's way of life. The tribes dominating the driest regions of the Great Plains included the Cheyenne, the Arapaho, the Comanche, the Kiowa, and the Teton Sioux (Lakota). These traveling hunters took their skin-covered tepees with them as they followed the trail of buffalo, antelope, elk, and deer.

A few tribes—among them the Mandan, the Hidatsa, the Pawnee, and the Omaha—occupied relatively fertile regions of the Plains. These farming peoples raised a variety of crops, lived in lodges with solid-earth walls, and used tepees only when going on a hunt. On the eastern edge of the Plains lived the Santee Sioux (Dakota) and the Plains Ojibway, groups that both farmed and hunted.

Two scouts cross the Great Plains
on horseback.

Whatever the patterns of their daily lives, the Plains Indians tried to follow the traditions of their ancestors. Older tribal members taught the young in the great school of the outdoors, counseling them to live in harmony with nature, or Mother Earth. The Indians believed that all of creation had spiritual powers. Plants and animals were viewed as gifts from God, whom the Indians called the Great Spirit. Meant to support life, these gifts were not to be destroyed needlessly. So the Plains Indians took from the earth only what they needed for their daily lives. They strove to keep their lands fertile and their streams clear. And, in time-honored rituals, they thanked the Great Spirit for the abundance of the earth.

Tribal members generally cooperated with one another for their economic well-being. As Sioux historian Vine Deloria wrote in Custer Died for Your Sins:

> In the old days a tribe suffered and prospered as a unity. When the hunting was good, everyone ate, when it was bad, everyone suffered. Never was the tribe overbalanced economically so that half would always starve and half would thrive. In this sense, all tribal members had a guaranteed annual income.

The Plains Indians did not hoard wealth for its own sake, an action that would imply a mistrust of the Great Spirit. The wealthy were more likely to win respect by giving to the poor. The Plains groups believed that people should be judged by who they are rather than by what they own.

The extended family was of great importance to the Plains Indians. In many cases, several generations lived together in the same dwelling, sharing the work and income. This arrangement gave growing children a sense of security, for there were many people to offer support and guidance. Youngsters knew what was expected of them and continually strove to win the approval of their elders. For this reason, there was little need to discipline children.

One of the most respected members of the tribe was the medicine man, or **shaman.** This healer knew how to set and fuse broken bones and how to cut out arrowheads from a wound and stop the bleeding. Using both herbs and drugs made from wild plants, the shaman could reduce pain and prevent infection. The Plains Indians believed that their healers were inspired by supernatural powers. A patient's strong faith in these powers often helped the shaman's cures to succeed.

Each tribe had a police force to keep order and warriors to protect land. Boys were taught to respect the skills and bravery of warriors from a very young age. In fact, tribal members considered it an honor for a warrior to die in battle. But the Plains Indians did not generally wage war to acquire new territory. Instead, they fought to defend their hunting grounds from invasion, to demonstrate their bravery, or to avenge a death or an injustice.

Most of the Plains Indians did not approve of killing for its own sake. Among many tribes, **counting coup**—the touching of a live enemy in battle—was more highly valued than **scalping**. Many present-day Indians believe that white people have overemphasized the role of the warrior in Native American life. As Arapaho historian Tom Shakespeare wrote in The Sky People:

> They [whites] tended to ignore or disregard the fact that the Indian warrior they would meet on Tuesday was out hunting on Wednesday, home with his family on Thursday, making and repairing tools on Friday, moving or trading on Saturday, lounging in the shade on Sunday, dancing or worshiping on Monday.

Until white settlers came to the Plains, Indian warfare was limited to raids by small war parties against enemy camps. But the fighting strategies of white people vastly increased warfare on the Plains in the 1800s. The fighting tactics of some tribes could be brutal, but white soldiers often fought to eliminate entire Indian camps. There was nothing in the Indian world, in fact, to match the armies and the weapons that the white people used to gain control of the Plains.

By 1890 the wars for the Great Plains had ended. Indian resistance came to a halt, and the greatest Indian leaders were dead or imprisoned. "Nothing lives long, except the earth and the mountains." So sang White Antelope, chief of the Cheyenne, just before U.S. soldiers shot him. Indian villages lay in ruins. The U.S. Army forced survivors onto barren **reservations,** where people were deprived of food, health care, and a means of making a living.

These hardships nearly crushed the Indian spirit. Someone once said, though, that you can take away a peoples' freedom but not their memories. Behind the wire fences of the reservations, some of the elders began to speak of how life had been when they were free. In telling of the old ways, they relived the past and helped to preserve their traditions for future generations.

These tribal historians possessed extraordinary powers of perception and memory, and their narratives aroused wide public interest, especially among writers and translators. In the late nineteenth and early twentieth centuries, historical and autobiographical accounts by Indians began to appear in books and magazines. A Native American literary tradition emerged, taking its place alongside an ancient and honored oral heritage. These writings not only provide insight into the nineteenth-century Indian experience, but also convey the diversity and the cultural richness of the peoples of the Great Plains.

Chapter 1

Charles A. Eastman

Indian historian Charles Alexander Eastman was born in 1858 near Redwood Falls, Minnesota. A member of the Santee (Dakota) branch of the Sioux Nation,[1] his Indian name was Ohiyesa. His mother died in childbirth. His father, a warrior, was captured by white soldiers during the U.S.-Dakota Conflict of 1862 and presumed dead by family members.

According to custom, relatives adopted Ohiyesa. His uncle taught him the skills necessary for survival in the wilderness—self-discipline, sharpening of the senses, and the strategies of the **warpath** and the hunt. Ohiyesa's grandmother also influenced his life. A wise woman, she gave Ohiyesa the high ideals that molded his life.

When Ohiyesa was fifteen years old, his father suddenly returned—not from the dead but from imprisonment. The father had converted to the Christian religion and had accepted the white peoples' way of life. He encouraged his son to follow a similar direction. Ohiyesa quickly made the transition to white society, taking the name Charles Eastman. He graduated from Dartmouth College in New Hampshire and later won wide recognition as a physician, lecturer, and author. Throughout his life, Eastman devoted himself to preserving Sioux culture and tradition. His autobiography, Indian Boyhood, relates his youthful adventures, providing a wealth of information about the values and customs of his people.

A creek winds through a snow-covered forest in Minnesota. Some Sioux hunted and fished in this region, which borders the prairies of the Great Plains.

Selections from
Indian Boyhood

The Freest Life in the World

What boy would not be an Indian for a while when he thinks of the freest life in the world? This life was mine. Every day there was a real hunt. There was real game. Occasionally, there was a medicine dance away off in the woods where no one could disturb us, in which [we] boys impersonated [our] elders, Brave Bull, Standing Elk, High Hawk, Medicine Bear, and the rest. [We] painted and imitated [our] fathers and grandfathers to the minutest detail and accurately, too, because [we] had seen the real thing all [our] lives.

We were not only good mimics, but we were close students of nature. We studied the habits of animals just as you study your books. We watched the men of our people and represented them in our play, then learned to emulate them in our lives.

No people have a better use of their five senses than the children of the wilderness. We could smell as well as [we could] hear and see. We could feel and taste as well as we could see and hear. Nowhere has the memory been more fully developed than in the wildlife, and I can still see wherein I owe much to my early training....

Indian children were trained so that they hardly ever cried much in the night. This was very expedient and necessary in their exposed life. In my infancy, it was my grandmother's custom to put me to sleep, as she said, with the birds, and to waken me with them, until it became a habit....An Indian must always rise early. In the first place, as a hunter, he finds his game best at daybreak. Secondly, other tribes, when on the warpath, usually make their attack very early in the morning....We like to rise before daybreak, in order to travel when the air is cool and when unobserved, perchance, by our enemies.

As a little child, it was instilled into me to be silent and reticent (reserved). [These were two] of the most important traits to form in the character of the Indian. As a hunter and warrior, [they were] considered absolutely necessary to him and [were] thought to lay the foundations of patience and self-control. There are times when boisterous mirth is indulged in by our people, but the rule is gravity and decorum.

In winter, the Sioux and other Indians of the northern Great Plains strapped on snowshoes to help them walk in deep snow.

After all, my babyhood was full of interest and the beginnings of life's realities. The spirit of daring was already whispered into my ears. The value of the eagle feather as worn by the warrior had caught my eye. One day, when I was left alone at scarcely two years of age, I took my uncle's **warbonnet** and plucked out all its eagle feathers to decorate my dog and myself. So soon the life that was about me had made its impress, and already I desired intensely to comply with all of its demands.

An Indian Boy's Training

It is commonly supposed that there is no systematic education of their children among the **aborigines** of this country. Nothing could be farther from the truth....

The expectant parents conjointly bent all their efforts to the task of giving the newcomer the best they could gather from a long line of ancestors. A pregnant Indian woman would often choose one of the greatest characters of her family and tribe as a model for her child. This hero was daily called to mind. She would gather from tradition all of [the person's] noted deeds and daring exploits, rehearsing them to herself when alone....

The Indians believed, also, that certain kinds of animals would confer peculiar gifts upon the unborn, while others would leave so strong an adverse impression that the child might become a monstrosity....Even the meat of certain animals was denied the pregnant woman because it was supposed to influence the disposition or features of the child.

Scarcely was the embryo warrior ushered into the world, when he was met by lullabies that speak of wonderful exploits in hunting and war. Those ideas which so fully occupied his mother's mind before his birth are now put into words....He is called the future defender of his people, whose lives may depend upon his courage and skill. If the child is a girl, she is at once addressed as the future mother of a noble race.

In hunting songs, the leading animals are introduced. They come to the boy to offer their bodies for the sustenance of his tribe. The animals are regarded as his friends and spoken of...as his cousins, grandfathers, and grandmothers. The songs of wooing, adapted as lullabies, were equally imaginative, and the suitors were often animals personified, while pretty maidens were represented by the mink and the doe.

Very early the Indian boy assumed the task of preserving and transmitting the legends of his ancestors and his race. Almost every evening, a myth or a true story of some deed done in the past was narrated by one of the parents or grandparents while the boy listened with parted lips and glistening eyes. On the following evening, he was usually required to repeat it. If he was not an apt scholar, he struggled long with his task. But, as a rule, the Indian boy is a good listener and has a good memory, so that the stories were tolerably well mastered. The members of the household became his audience, by which he was alternately criticized and applauded.

This sort of teaching at once enlightens the boy's mind and stimulates his ambition. His conception of his own future career becomes a vivid and irresistible force. Whatever there is for him to learn must be learned. Whatever qualifications are necessary to [be] a truly great man, he must seek at any expense of danger and hardship. Such was the feeling of the imaginative and brave young Indian. It became apparent to him in early life that he must accustom himself to rove alone and not to fear or dislike the impression of solitude.

It seems to be a popular idea that all the characteristic skill of the Indian is instinctive and hereditary. This is a mistake. All of the stoicism and patience of the Indian are acquired traits, and continual practice alone makes him master of the art of woodcraft. Physical training and dieting were not neglected. I remember that I was not allowed to have beef soup or any warm drink. The soup was for the old men. General rules for the young were never to take their food very hot, nor to drink much water.

My uncle, who educated me up to the age of fifteen years, was a strict disciplinarian and a good teacher. When I left the tepee in the morning, he would say, "Hakadah, look closely to everything you see." And at evening, on my return, he used often to catechize (question) me for an hour. "On which side of the trees is the lighter-colored bark? On which side do they have the most regular branches?"

It was his custom to let me name all the new birds that I had seen during the day. I would name them according to the color or the shape of the bill or their song or the appearance and locality of the nest—in fact, anything about the bird that impressed me as characteristic. I made many ridiculous errors, I must admit. He then usually informed me of the correct name. Occasionally I made a hit, and this he would warmly commend.

He went much deeper into this science when I was a little older, that is, about the age of eight or nine years. He would say, for instance:

"How do you know that there are fish in yonder lake?"

"Because they jump out of the water for flies at midday."

He would smile at my prompt but superficial reply. "What do you think of the little pebbles grouped together under the shallow water? And what made the pretty curved marks in the sandy bottom and the little sandbanks? Where do you find the fish-eating birds? Have the inlet and the outlet of a lake have anything to do with the question?"

He did not expect a correct reply at once to all the voluminous questions that he put to me on these occasions, but he meant to make me observant and a good student of nature.

"Hakadah," he would say to me, "you ought to follow the example of the *shunktokecha* (wolf). Even when he is surprised and runs for his life, he will pause to take one more look at you before he enters his final retreat. So you must take a second look at everything you see.

"It is better to view animals unobserved. I have been a witness to their courtships and their quarrels and have learned many of their secrets in this way. I was once the unseen spectator of a thrilling battle between a pair of grizzly bears and three buffalo—a rash act for the bears, for it was in the Moon of Strawberries, when the buffalo sharpen and polish their horns for bloody contests among themselves.

"I advise you, my boy, never to approach a grizzly's den from the front, but to steal up behind and throw your blanket or a stone in front of the hole. He does not usually rush for it but first puts his head out and listens and then comes out very indifferently and sits on his haunches on the mound in front of the hole before he makes any attack. While he is exposing himself in this fashion, aim at his heart. Always be as cool as the animal himself." Thus he armed me against the cunning of the savage beasts by teaching me how to outwit them.

"In hunting," he would resume, "you will be guided by the habits of the animal you seek. Remember that a moose stays in swampy or low land between high mountains near a spring or lake for thirty to sixty days at a time. Most large game moves about continually, except the doe in the spring—it is then a very easy matter to find her with the fawn. Conceal yourself in a convenient place as soon as you observe any signs of the presence of either, and then call with your birchen doe-caller.

"Whichever one hears you first will soon appear in your neighborhood. But you must be very watchful, or you may be made a fawn of by a large wildcat. They understand the characteristic call of the doe perfectly well.

"When you have any difficulty with a bear or a wildcat—that is, if the creature shows signs of attacking you—you must make him fully understand that you have seen him and are aware of his intentions. If you are not well equipped for a pitched battle, the only way to make him retreat is to take a long, sharp-pointed pole for a spear and rush toward him. No wild beast will face this unless he is cornered and already wounded. These fierce beasts are generally afraid of the common weapon of the larger animals—the horns, and if these are very long and sharp, they dare not risk an open fight.

"There is one exception to this rule—[gray wolves] will attack fiercely when very hungry. But their courage depends upon their numbers. In this they are like white men. One wolf or two will never attack a man. They will stampede a herd of buffaloes in order to get at the calves. They will rush upon a herd of antelopes, for these are helpless. But they are always careful about attacking man." Of this nature were the instructions of my uncle, who was widely known at that time as among the greatest hunters of his tribe.

All boys were expected to endure hardship without complaint. In...warfare, a young man must, of course, be an athlete and used to undergoing all sorts of privations. He must be able to go without food and water for two or three days without displaying any weakness or to run for a day and a night without any rest. He must be able to traverse a pathless and wild country without losing his way either in the day or nighttime. He cannot refuse to do any of these things if he aspires to be a warrior.

Sometimes my uncle would waken me very early in the morning and challenge me to fast (go without food) with him all day. I had to accept the challenge. We blackened our faces with charcoal so that every boy in the village would know that I was fasting for the day. Then the little tempters would make my life a misery until the merciful sun hid behind the western hills.

I can scarcely recall the time when my stern teacher began to give sudden war whoops (loud cries) over my head in the morning while I was sound asleep. He expected me to leap up with perfect presence of mind, always ready to grasp a weapon of some sort and to give a shrill whoop in reply....Often he would vary these tactics by shooting off his gun just outside of the lodge while I was yet asleep, at the same time giving bloodcurdling yells. After a time, I became used to this.

When Indians went upon the warpath, it was their custom to try the new warriors thoroughly before coming to an engagement. For instance, when they were near a hostile camp, they would select the novices to go after the water and make them do all sorts of things to prove their courage. In accordance with this idea, my uncle used to send me off after water when we camped after dark in a strange place. Perhaps the country was full of wild beasts, and, for aught I knew, there might be scouts from hostile bands of Indians lurking in that very neighborhood.

Yet I never objected, for that would show cowardice. I picked my way through the woods, dipped my pail in the water, and hurried back, always careful to make as little noise as a cat. Being only a boy, my heart would leap at every crackling of a dry twig or distant hooting of an owl, until, at last, I reached our tepee. Then my uncle would perhaps say, "Ah, Hakadah, you are a thorough warrior," empty out the precious contents of the pail, and order me to go a second time.

Imagine how I felt! But I wished to be a brave man.... Silently I would take the pail and endeavor to retrace my footsteps in the dark.

With all this, our manners and morals were not neglected. I was made to respect the adults and especially the aged. I was not allowed to join in their discussions, nor even to speak in their presence, unless requested to do so. Indian etiquette was very strict, and among the requirements was that of avoiding direct address. A term of relationship (such as grandfather) or some title of courtesy was commonly used instead of the personal name by those who wished to show respect. We were taught generosity to the poor and reverence for the "Great Mystery."[3] Religion was the basis of all Indian training.

Chapter 2

John Stands In Timber

The Sioux gave the Cheyenne their name, which means "people of a different speech" in the Siouan language. But the ancient tribal name of the Cheyenne was Tsistsistas, meaning "beautiful people." The Cheyenne, a deeply religious and traditional group, originally farmed territory in present-day Minnesota and later migrated to the banks of the Missouri River in what are now North and South Dakota.

In the late 1700s, the Cheyenne learned to ride horses, and their way of life changed. They became hunters, following the buffalo and living on the trail. At the same time, the Sioux, who were searching for new hunting grounds, began pushing the Cheyenne farther south. About 1832 the Cheyenne split into two groups, both of which played vital roles in the wars for control of the Great Plains. Today the Northern Cheyenne are based in Montana, and many Southern Cheyenne live in Oklahoma.

The Cheyenne tribal historian John Stands In Timber spent a lifetime learning the history and lore of his people. Beginning in 1956, when he was in his seventies, he dictated a long and remarkable narrative to an anthropologist named Margot Liberty.

Entitled Cheyenne Memories, the narrative contains John Stands In Timber's personal account of Cheyenne history. The Indian historian describes Cheyenne social life and customs, the organization of the Cheyenne government, and the structure of the Cheyenne military. More importantly, John Stands In Timber brings into sharp focus the Cheyenne reverence for sacred traditions and respect for law.

Under a stormy sky, a herd of buffalo feeds on tall prairie grasses.

Selections from
Cheyenne Memories

Law Comes to the Cheyenne

When I was just a little boy, I began to listen to old men and women of the Cheyenne tribe telling stories that had been handed down from earlier generations. Many of [these older people] used to visit my grandparents who raised me—my parents died before I was ten years old. And I could listen and listen. If they talked all day, I would be there the whole time.

I memorized some of the stories that way. And when I came back from school in 1905, I thought I would write some of them down, so I went back to these old people to get the details straight. I have been doing it ever since. That is why the Cheyenne call me their historian, both the Southerners in Oklahoma and the Northerners in Montana. There is still much to learn. I talk to old-timers and their sons and daughters whenever I can, getting it straight about this or that battle and other things that happened long ago. But the real old-timers are dead now, and I am old. I have helped many others to collect our history. Now I am glad to finish a book of my own, with all the Indian stories in one place.

An old storyteller would smooth the ground in front of him with his hand and make two marks in it with his right thumb, two with his left, and a double mark with both thumbs together. Then he would rub his hands and pass his right hand up his right leg to his waist and touch his left hand and pass it on up his right arm to his breast. He did the same thing with his left and right hands going up the other side. Then he touched the marks on the ground with both hands and rubbed them together and passed them over his head and all over his body.

That meant the Creator had made human beings' bodies and their limbs as he had made the earth and that the Creator was witness to what was to be told. [The storytellers] did not tell any of the old or holy stories without that. And it was a good thing. I always trusted them, and I believe they told the truth.

Now I am one of the last people who knows some of these things. I am telling them as they were told to me during more than eighty years among the Cheyenne people. I can tell only what I know. But I have not added anything or left anything out.

The old Cheyenne could not write things down.[1] They had to keep everything in their heads and tell it to their children so the history of the tribe would not be forgotten. There were tales of the Creation and the early days before the Cheyenne lived in the Plains country. Many of these have been forgotten, but some have lasted to this day. And there were tales of the hero Sweet Medicine, the savior of the Cheyenne tribe, who gave us our laws and way of living....

Many centuries ago, the prophet and savior Sweet Medicine came to the prairie people. Before his birth, the people were bad, living without law and killing one another. But with his life those things changed. Indians are often called savages, and it was true of the Cheyenne at first but not after Sweet Medicine's time....

Sweet Medicine organized the soldiers and the chiefs and then taught them about the Sacred Arrows[2] and the laws of the tribe. These things were all thought of together—one could not exist without the others. They were begun together, and they are together in the minds of the Cheyenne people even now. The Cheyenne say that the eagle on the American silver dollar is the emblem of their chiefs and that [the bird] is holding the four arrows to prove that what Sweet Medicine brought is not dead.

I would like to go back now and tell about the chiefs' organization and duties....The chiefs were the real power of the tribe, and their organization ceremony still follows the pattern that Sweet Medicine taught them.[3] It was connected with the Arrows, as I have said, giving it a religious feeling, and also with the Chiefs' Medicine, which Sweet Medicine brought with the Arrows from the Holy Mountain. He carried [the medicine] himself through his lifetime and later put it in the care of a keeper, the man chosen to be the Old Man Chief or fifth of the Head Chiefs.[4]

At the first chiefs' organization, Sweet Medicine named the four who would take the positions of head chief in this first ceremony, and also the one who would act as keeper of the Chiefs' Medicine at the swearing-in. [Sweet Medicine] had four sticks prepared, representing the four chiefs and the forty in the membership. Then he took the five men he had chosen into the Arrow tepee. There he seated them and prepared a pipe, filling it with kinnikinnick (a mixture of dried leaves and bark) and tobacco and placing sweet grass incense on top. The Chiefs' Medicine was unwrapped

In their free time, the Cheyenne entertained themselves with a variety of games, including javelin throwing, wrestling, kickball, stone tossing, and stick-in-the-hoop.

and reverently touched to the top of the loaded pipe. The first head chief, sitting at the right of the tepee, was called forward, and Sweet Medicine showed him how to hold the pipe for a minute, with both hands on its stem. Then the chief smoked two or three puffs and returned to his place.

The other three head chiefs also smoked in this manner. Then the Keeper of the Medicine received the pipe and took it to the first chief at the doorway and returned to his own seat at the rear. The first head chief smoked

A Cheyenne chief addresses a tribal council.

it again, and then passed it to the next man, and so it went until it had been around the circle. Next a new pipe was prepared and offered to three more men brought in by Sweet Medicine, one to serve as Keeper of the Arrows and two as servants of the chiefs' council. After they had smoked, the balance of the chiefs' membership was filled out to make forty-four in all plus the Keeper of the Medicine. And after all had smoked, Sweet Medicine's instructions began.

He told them there had been a band that called itself soldiers, and these men controlled the people. They killed many men who objected to them or disobeyed their orders. Now he said there would be no more of that. Anyone who killed his kinsman—his tribesman—would be cast out. If he gave himself up in a good way, the military societies would take him out across four ridges or four rivers and leave him there. After he was turned loose, he was considered an enemy—anyone could kill him. But if he was still alive after four years he could come back to the village. The Sacred Arrow Priest could meet him and perform a ceremony of re-adoption. But Sweet Medicine ordered that he would not be free to do all things. He could not go to public gatherings or any religious ceremony or entertainment. People should not eat with him, but if he made a visit give him a separate dish. And if he had children after committing this murder they would also be outlawed on account of their father.

"Listen to me carefully and truthfully follow up my instructions," Sweet Medicine told the chiefs. "You chiefs are peacemakers. Though your son might be killed in front of your tepee, you should make a peace pipe and smoke. Then you would be called an honest chief. You chiefs own the land and the people. If your men, your soldier societies, should be scared and retreat, you are not to step back but take a stand to protect your land and your people. Get out and talk to the people. If strangers come, you are the ones to give presents to them and invitations. When you meet someone or he comes to your tepee asking for anything, give it to him. Never refuse. Go outside your tepee and sing your chief's song, so all the people know you have done something good."

As closely as I can put it, this is what he told them. And the chiefs did keep it in their minds. When I was a boy they used to go up on a hill near camp and talk to the people about all the laws Sweet Medicine had taught

During the 1800s, the Cheyenne were famous for their fierce warriors and daring war tactics. Although they did not invite conflict, the Cheyenne fought many battles against white settlers and U.S. soldiers. As a result, the Cheyenne were among the last of the Plains Indians to surrender their lands and their freedom.

so long ago. There were many of them. The Cheyenne were not supposed to marry too young or to anyone related to them. They have forgotten that today. They were not to take anything by force from another person, or use it without permission, or to say bad things about others, especially the leaders or chiefs. They were to take pride in their bodies and the way they appeared, to keep clean and stay healthy...

I learned the laws from my grandfather. He made me remember them. He told me about fights. A number of times I could have gotten into them, but he used to say there was always someone ready to be jealous and

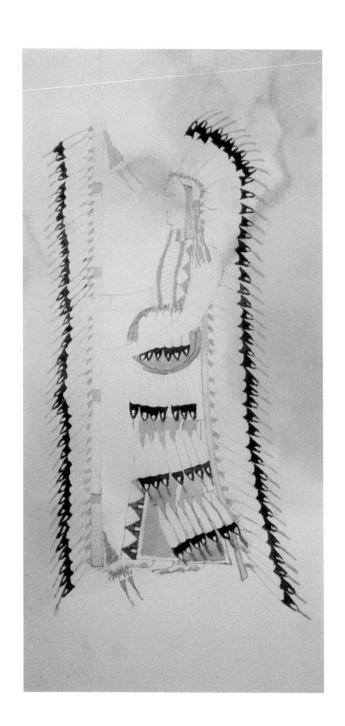

A Cheyenne artist painted this portrait of a chief wearing a warbonnet. Each of the black-tipped eagle feathers decorating the headdress represents a feat of bravery.

wanting to fight or argue. "Don't give him one word," he would tell me, "even if he should call you bad things. Walk away from him. After a time, that man will come back and be one of your best friends." And it is true. I have done it many times.

Sweet Medicine's Prophecy

"My friends," [Sweet Medicine] said, "once I was young and able, but a man lives only a short time, and now I am old and helpless and ready to leave you. I have brought you many things sent by the gods for your use. You live the way I have taught you and follow the laws. You must not forget them, for they have given you strength and the ability to support yourselves and your families.

"There is a time coming, though, when many things will change. Strangers called Earth Men will appear among you. Their skins are light-colored, and their ways are powerful. They clip their hair short and speak no Indian tongue. Follow nothing these Earth Men do, but keep your own ways that I have taught you as long as you can.

"The buffalo will disappear, at last, and another animal will take its place, a slick animal with a long tail and split hoofs, whose flesh you will learn to eat. But first there will be another animal you must learn to use. It has a shaggy neck and a tail almost touching the ground. Its hoofs are round. This animal will carry you on his back and help you in many ways. Those far hills that seem only a blue vision in the distance take many days to reach now, but with this animal you can get there in a short time, so fear him not. Remember what I have said.

"But at last you will not remember. Your ways will change. You will leave your religion for something new. You will lose respect for your leaders and start quarreling with one another. You will lose track of your relations and marry women from your own families. You will take after the Earth Men's ways and forget good things by which you have lived and in the end become worse than crazy.

"I am sorry to say these things, but I have seen them, and you will find that they come true."

The people were all quiet, thinking of what Sweet Medicine had said. But they did not believe him. At last they left him there alone, and he was not seen again.

Cheyenne on a reservation wait for U.S. government officials to distribute flour, sugar, and meat. The Indians, who were not allowed to leave the reservation to hunt, depended on these supplies for survival.

Chapter 3

Two Leggings

During the nineteenth century, the Crow made their homes among the rocky slopes and canyons of the Yellowstone River Valley in what is now Montana and northern Wyoming. Many other hunting groups raided the Crow lands, which were rich in wild game and natural resources. For this reason, the Crow often battled enemy invaders, the most aggressive of which were the Blackfeet and the Sioux. For the Crow, success on the warpath was the quickest route to honor.

The Crow relied heavily on divine spirits for protection and guidance in battle. Before going on the warpath, for example, a young Crow warrior purified himself and awaited a vision. The youth believed that if he was fortunate, supernatural powers would reveal to him the proper strategy for the raid. Many Plains tribes performed the Sun Dance, a religious ritual meant to strengthen their vital powers and to renew the earth. But only the Crow performed the Sun Dance to ask for support in their revenge against enemies.

Two Leggings was a Crow warrior and military leader of minor rank. Beginning in the year 1919, in both his native tongue and in sign language, he recounted the events of his battle-scarred life to a white man, William Wildschut. In 1923, when the manuscript for Two Leggings: The Making of a Crow Warrior, was completed, Two Leggings was approximately eighty years old. Two Leggings describes his lifelong struggle to fulfill the military ideals of his tribe. He also tells of his unsatisfied quest for a vision important enough to win him high status among the Crow.

At the western edge of the Great Plains,
mountains border a rocky plateau.

Selections from
Two Leggings:
The Making of a Crow Warrior

First War Party

I was growing restless shooting rabbits and longed to join the war parties I watched going out. In the evenings, I wandered through the village until I found a tepee where some old man was telling stories of famous raids. If I was not invited in, I would sit outside, my ear pressed to the skin wall. Later that night, in my brother's tepee, I would imagine those same things happening to me. When I asked my brother to let me join a raiding party, he only laughed but watched closely to make sure I did not run off.

I was fourteen years old when we were camped on Bear Creek, a tributary of the Musselshell River, near where it empties into Big River. One day I heard that Shows His Wing, Two Belly, and Bank were leading a war party to recover some horses stolen by the Piegans.[1] My brother would not give me his permission to go, which I knew Shows His Wing would require....

I strolled to the edge of the tepees, carrying my bow and arrows. When my brother turned around, I ran behind a tepee and into the bushes. Arriving at the top of a nearby ridge, I hid behind some rocks while the war party walked by.

I was afraid to join right away but showed myself when they stopped for their noon meal. Shows His Wing asked what I was doing, and I answered that I wanted to be their helper. He said I was too young and chose four men to take me home. Although I begged, my words were like the wind to him.

When we could see our village, they told me to go on alone. I sat on the ground, watching them disappear over the ridge. Then I looked at our tepees. If I returned, I would never have a chance to improve my life. I would rather be killed on a raid than do nothing in camp. I ran until I saw the four men again and started walking slowly behind. When they reached their camp at nightfall, I hid as close as I dared.

It was late in Leaf-Falling Moon, and snow covered the ground. As I watched their fires, my feet grew numb, but I was only worried whether Shows His Wing would let me stay. The men had built four shelters of tree branches covered with brush and blankets, and I could hear them talking inside. When someone walked out of the firelight, I did not think he would see me, but the clouds parted and the full moon lit the country like day. I had to answer when he called, and he led me to Shows His Wing. The men were resting after their meal and told me to cut a piece of fresh elk and broil it. As Shows His Wing watched me eat, he kept saying that they were walking far and I was so small.

I did not feel that small, but he told his men they should have taken me into the village. When I finished eating, Bob Tail Wolf and Wolf Cap accompanied me back a second time. But at dawn, when we reached the location of their last noon camp, they said I knew the way.

Again I waited until they had disappeared, and again I walked in their tracks. Soon I found the remains of their fire and built it up to warm my feet. It dried my moccasins but made me fall asleep. When I woke it was sundown....I followed [the war party's] tracks in the moonlight, walking across ice, through groves of cottonwoods, and along the riverbanks.

When we are young, we are all cowards. I was alone for the first time that night, and the owls scared me. Stopping for a moment, I would hear strange noises and start to run.

Soon I smelled cooked meat and knew I was close. I was afraid to get too near, but once again someone noticed me and took me to...Shows His Wing. [He] said that I was like a coyote trailing behind their party. Boys are always looking for excitement, he said, and his men should have taken me directly to my brother's tepee. But since I had shown my eagerness to go, he allowed me to stay. I was happy and could not speak.

A fat buffalo had been killed, and Shows His Wing told me to eat. When he learned I had only a spare pair of my brother's moccasins, he told me to throw away those and my own torn pair. Then he asked some men for extra moccasins but none fit, so he cut down my brother's pair and sewed them up again....In the morning, Shows His Wing led us where he thought the Piegans had gone, and we soon found their tracks.

The men were watching to see if I got tired. But I had trained myself and even kept up when we ran one entire night because...we were catching up. The following sunset we sighted their group of brush shelters.

Our party consisted of only six experienced warriors, two younger men, and myself. We three were told to stay behind, and when it grew dark the others crawled out. After they had left, I tried to persuade the young men to join me, but they said they were too young for real fighting.

I was excited and also began crawling out. When our men stopped to spread out, I lay behind them. It was nearly daybreak when they noticed me, whispering that I must get back. But I was a man now and wanted to see what kind of people these Piegans were.

White Buffalo thought it was too dangerous, and someone else warned that if the Piegans chased us I must not cry out. Then Does Not Turn Back said that I might be braver than any of them and remembered how well I had run. He told me to stay by him.

By the time the sun touched the treetops, we had surrounded their camp. I was told again to go back, but I stayed, holding tightly to my bow and

Mounted on horseback, a Crow war party brings news of the enemy to a war council.

A sunset silhouettes an Indian hunter.

arrows. However, the Piegans had discovered us and had slipped away. We quickly picked up the trail and soon saw seven men riding [the stolen] horses toward the mountains. Then they dropped out of sight.

Shows His Wing led us on a shortcut across the hills, arriving at the mountain pass at sunset. [The Piegans] had not yet crossed, and we hid among the trees. Since he was not expecting the Piegans for a while, Shows His Wing told us to rest. But I could not sleep. While I watched the pass, a dog we had brought to carry our few belongings lay next to me.

When it lifted its nose and began growling, I looked closer. Men walked out of the darkness, and I put an arrow on my bow. I heard the heavy breathing of my friends sleeping behind me but never thought to wake them up.

The dog barked, someone shouted, and the Piegans ran down the hillside. Our men were awake and running in the opposite direction, but three stood with me, waiting to see if more Piegans showed. We saw none, and it was too dark to follow into the thick timber. Breath (one of the elder warriors) was with me, and he yelled for the others to pick up their blankets.

When they crowded around, I spoke with a serious face, telling them that one man had walked right up to me and that when he felt my arrow he had screamed. Then I had looked around and only three were with me. Someone said that they had been trying to send me home and now I had proved myself the bravest....

We returned [home] a few days later, and my brother scolded me as soon as I walked into his tepee. But he must have heard how I had behaved because after that he did not treat me like the small boy he had always known. Although on that first war party we did not fight or steal horses, it was the beginning of a new life.

The Vision Quest

During the snow season, we camped on Arrow Creek, but when the snow melted and the ice left the rivers we moved to Dry Head Creek between Arrow Creek and the Bighorn River. Soon after our tepees were pitched, eight of us left camp to fast in the Bighorn Mountains, planning to climb a mountain on the east side of Black Canyon called Where The Thunderbird Sits Down Mountain.

Most of our people were afraid of this place because it was the Thunderbird's[2] home. Long ago a man named Covers Himself With The Grass was traveling through this country. He heard a strange noise and looked up to see the Thunderbird flying down. His horse bucked, and when he dismounted, it ran off. With his rawhide rope, he tied himself to a tree at the canyon bottom. The rush of air from the Thunderbird's wings was so strong the trees on both sides were uprooted. Covers Himself With The Grass was saved, but his tree was thrown about until he was sure it would pull up.

We decided to fast [in the Bighorn Mountains] because we wanted a stronger medicine.[3] Medicine Crow, Young Mountain, Mouse Walks, Shows His Tail, and I were all close friends, but Young Rabbit, Plenty Screeching Owl, and Yellow Weasel were nearly strangers to us.

Each man carried his own robe painted with white clay. When we reached the foot of the mountain we took a sweat bath and cleaned ourselves. Building a fire, we purified our bodies in sweet-sage smoke and then painted ourselves with white clay. We arrived at the [mountain's peak] before dark…

I asked Young Mountain to help me sacrifice my flesh, and he lifted the skin on my left arm, cutting out a piece that looked like a horse track. I hoped to steal horses and had asked for that cut. Then I faced east, held the piece up to the sky, and told the Great Above Person that I wished for some animal to eat this and help me receive a powerful medicine. I also asked for a long life....

Stretching out on my back, I watched the moon and stars by night and followed the sun through the next day. As I prayed, I grew very thirsty.

After the second night, five men wanted to return home. I did not think about giving in and let them leave. Medicine Crow and Young Mountain also stayed on. We told the returning men to kill an elk at the foot of the mountain, to cache (hide) the meat, and then to tell our families we were staying all four nights.[4]

A strange noise rushing up the mountainside woke me early the third day. Immediately I thought of the Thunderbird and grew afraid. As [the noise] drew near, I pulled my robe around me. I felt better when it proved to be a hailstorm and cut leafy branches to protect myself. Then all became

The Crow and other Plains Indians chased buffalo on swift horses. The galloping animals allowed the hunters to use their spears or bows and arrows at close range.

quiet again. I lay and thought of all the animals of this earth, praying that the Great Above Person would lead one to me in my sleep, that it would eat my flesh and become my sacred helper for the rest of my life.

All the next day I watched the sky and slept....That night the vision of my last fast came again. When I woke, it was nearly dawn, but one bright star shone above the eastern horizon. After I saw it, I covered my head with my robe and fell asleep again. [In my vision,] a man appeared above the horizon, and a voice which I could not locate spoke to me....A hawk perched on a hoop on his head. Something red in the right side of the man's hair grew larger and finally colored the entire sky....The man asked if I knew the name of the bird on his head. I lay still without speaking. He said the name of the bird was The Bird Above All The Mountains.

In the future, he said, people would hear about me all over the earth. Then I learned my vision man's song: "Thank you. A long time going to be a chief.[5] Thank you again."

Behind me I heard a voice but saw no one else. It told me to look at that man on the horizon whose name was Looks All Over The Earth.

When I saw my vision man again, a large black eagle was flying over his head. The hoop where the hawk was sitting was painted partly blue, which meant the earth, partly yellow, which meant the day, and partly black, which meant the night. The man took off the hoop, looked at it, and told me to look around. After singing another song, he held the hoop before his eyes. Although he was seeing several visions, I saw nothing.

The other voice behind me said to look west and asked if I saw the trail. Through the hoop held before my eyes I had a vision of a trail running from the west, where the wind comes from, and heading east. At its end I saw a tepee and grazing horses. Between [the tepee and me], snow covered the ground. Then a big eagle flew over my head, and I noticed its claws. The voice behind me said to look toward the Musselshell River. Turning in that direction and looking through the hoop, I saw bodies on the ground. The eagle hung over them and pretended to grab one. My dream man sang: "Thank you. A long time going to be a chief. Thank you again...."

Then the voice behind me said to look east, where I saw a big sweat lodge[6] built of forty-four willows and four small sweat lodges of four branches each, all close to the Bighorn River where my future house would stand. Whenever I wanted to go on the warpath, the voice said, I must build those sweat lodges and sacrifice to him and his kind.

The sun was just rising as I woke. [I was] covered with perspiration. My blanket lay apart from me. Standing up, I thanked the Great Above Person for my vision and medicine. Young Mountain came over and asked if I wanted to stay. Since I had received my medicine, we left. I had felt weak and exhausted, but now my energy seemed to return. My arm had hurt, and I had lost much blood. But now I hardly noticed it.

Medicine Crow, Young Mountain, and I walked to the foot of the mountain where our five friends were waiting. After enjoying a meal of elk meat, we lit a pipe. Someone said that since this was the only time we could speak about our visions we should smoke this pipe and tell what had come to us.

When my turn came I smoked and...told about the horses but said I did not understand the snow's meaning. Young Mountain said we Crow knew less than half the earth people. To have them all know me meant something great.

Medicine Crow held the pipe and said he had seen a man and had dreamt a good dream. But then another spirit he could not see told him that the first man was a bad spirit who spoke lies. The second spirit then appeared as a man wearing a buffalo robe with the hair side out. But Medicine Crow could not see his face. Telling Medicine Crow to look toward the joining of the Little Bighorn and Bighorn Rivers, he said that something was shining over there. Medicine Crow was to remember this because when that thing would really be there, he would become a chief.

(Many years later, when Fort Custer was built near these rivers, we noticed how some windows shone in the light of the setting sun. Medicine Crow became a chief about the time the fort was completed.)

Young Mountain told Medicine Crow he did not think the vision very powerful. Mine had been best, he said, for the world was large, and if I became known all over that meant something powerful....

The rest had not dreamt anything, so we started back to camp, arriving at sunset. When my brother asked if I had received a vision, I said that I had, and he was pleased that now I would have better luck.

Chapter 4

Chief Luther Standing Bear

Luther Standing Bear was a hereditary chief[1] of the Oglala band of the Teton Sioux (Lakota). Born in 1868, he lived by the traditions of his people, who hunted the vast plains of South Dakota. After the U.S. government drove his tribe onto a reservation, however, he was sent east to Carlisle Indian School—a boarding school in Carlisle, Pennsylvania. At this school, Indians from many different tribes were taught English and learned the white peoples' way of life. Following graduation, Luther Standing Bear returned to the Rosebud Reservation in South Dakota, where he married, raised a family, and taught school.

Proud of his heritage, Chief Luther Standing Bear wrote many books depicting the Sioux traditional way of life before it was disrupted by whites. In My People, the Sioux, he vividly recalls the life of the hunter on the trail of the buffalo and reveals the cooperative spirit that prevailed in the Sioux family. He also tells of his education and respect for nature and the religious rituals that were a part of his everyday life. Chief Luther Standing Bear continues the narrative in Land of the Spotted Eagle, discussing Sioux religion and social customs and describing the Indians' close relationship to the earth.

In many places, the prairies of the Great Plains extend as far as the eye can see.

Selections from
My People, the Sioux and
Land of the Spotted Eagle

Home and Family

The Sioux nation to which I belong has always been very powerful. Many years ago, they traveled all over...hunting, camping, and enjoying life to its utmost in the many beautiful spots where they found the best wood and water.

It was in a cold winter, in the month when the bark of the trees cracked, in the year of "breaking up of camp," that I was born. I was the first son of Chief Standing Bear the First. In those days we had no calendars, no manner of keeping count of the days—only the month and the year were observed. Something of importance would, naturally, happen every year, and we kept track of the years in that manner. After I went to school and learned how to "count back," I learned that the year of "breaking camp" was A.D. 1868. The month when the bark of the trees cracked was December. Consequently, I was born in December 1868.

My mother was considered the most beautiful young woman among the Sioux at the time she married my father. Her name was Pretty Face. My grandfather—my father's father—was a chief and a very brave man. He had captured many spotted horses from other tribes....Therefore, when my father was born, he was given the name of Spotted Horse. This he kept until he was old enough to go on the warpath and earn his own name....

Our home life began in the tepee. It was there that we were born....A tepee would probably seem queer to a white child. But if you ever have a chance to live in one you will find it very comfortable—that is, if you get a *real* tepee, not the kind used by the moving-picture companies.

When I was a boy, all my tribe used tepees made of buffalo skins. Some were large, and others were quite small, depending upon the wealth of the owner. In my boyhood days, a man counted his wealth by the number of horses he owned. If a tepee was large, it took a great many poles to set it up and that called for a great many horses to move [the tepee] about when camp was broken....

My father's tepee was the largest in our tribe. When we made camp, all the rest of the tribe would camp at a distance, as they were afraid the wind might get too strong in the night and knock our tepee over on them.

At the top of the tepee were two flaps, which served as windbreaks. If the wind blew too hard from the north, then the flap on the north side was raised. If it came from the south, the south flap was raised. Our tepees were always set up facing the east, so we always had the west at our backs.

In case of rain, both flaps were closed down and tied to a stake driven in the ground. If a tepee was set up right, there never was any smoke inside, as the flue was open at the top. If snow fell heavily, it banked up all around the outside of the tepee, which helped keep us warm. On nights when there was a cold, sleeting rain, it was very pleasant to lie in bed and listen to the storm beating on the sides of the tepee. [The sound] even put us to sleep....In the center of the tepee, a large fire was built, and it was nice and warm, regardless of the weather outside....

We did not have very much [furniture in our tepees], but there was sufficient to keep us happy. We used no high bedsteads. We had a tripod tied together with a buckskin string. Straight branches were also strung to a buckskin thong, and these hung down in front of the tripod. These branches varied in size and were narrow at the top and wider at the bottom....On top of these small branches was hung a buffalo skin. This was fastened on top of the tripod....The branches kept the buffalo skin from sinking in between the two sticks of the tripod and served as a backrest. These tripods stood about five feet high. The skins were quite long, so that a portion of them trailed on the ground. In the center, another skin was laid. This made a very pretty bed and was fine to sleep in. The beds were made all around the sides of the tepee.

At the rear of the bed, against the tepee wall, a tanned hide was tied to the poles, on which was painted the history of the family. These were to the Indian what pictures were to the white man's home. This painted blanket could be worn as a robe when attending a dance.

At the back of the bed and in front of this painted skin, the woman of the house kept all the rawhide bags. These bags were very fancy affairs. They were made by the women. When a buffalo skin was brought in for painting, it was first staked to the ground and the women scraped all the meat off. The skin was then washed with water to make sure it was clean. While the skin was yet damp, it was painted. Our paints in those days were made from baked earth and berries. The paint pots were turtlebacks (turtle shells).

The Sioux used tall poles and buffalo hides to make their cone-shaped tepees. Openings at the tops of the tepees allowed smoke to escape from fires built inside the dwellings.

A woman prepares a buffalo hide by scraping and smoothing the surface.

The brush used by the artist was not really a brush but a small bone, rather ragged on the edge, so it would hold the paint. The straightedge, or ruler, was a very straight stick.

Then the woman who was to act as the artist got everything ready to decorate the hide. The paints were mixed with water. The woman kneeled on the skin and designed her patterns, putting in all the colors which she thought pretty and suited her fancy....

After the big bag was made, the scraps from the hide were used up. Some pieces were cut for moccasin soles. These were not painted. But the pieces which the women expected to make bags from were all painted at the same time as the big bag. The women made one little bag which served as a sort of workbox. In this the woman kept all the tools she needed in her sewing— the awl (a small, pointed tool used to make holes) and the sinews (animal tendons used as thread). She also made another [bag] to hold her comb. In those days, a comb was made from the tail of the porcupine. Another bag held paints and brushes. Sometimes knife cases were made from any of the leftover pieces of hide. All these were painted in pretty designs, and this work was always done by the women. The bag that held the warbonnet was also painted and decorated, but all war articles were painted by men....The bag that held the warbonnet always hung on the tripod of the bed. It never was laid on the ground.

Other bags, which held the clothing of the family, were decorated with dyed porcupine quills. These [bags] were made round from tanned buffalo skins. The woman cut out the size she desired, then sewed it with sinew, with buckskin tie-strings attached....When these round bags were in place on top of the rawhide bags, and the painted skin was hung up behind them, and the beds all made and a fire burning, the tepee looked just as neat as any white man's house.

When we were all settled for winter, our women fixed up the tepee as comfortably and inviting as possible. Not for Thanksgiving Day, for we were taught to give thanks every day. Not for Christmas or New Year's, because we knew nothing of these holidays of the white man. It was solely for our own pleasure and the assurance that we were safe for the long winter months.

[During the winter, the wild animals came to the Black Hills through a narrow passage known as Buffalo Gap] for protection from the icy blasts of winter. And the Sioux likewise went there. There were springs of clear water and plenty of wood. Nature seemed to hold us in her arms. And there we were contented to live in our humble tepees all through the rough winter.

After a time, of course, our tepees would begin to get old and worn. The poles would commence to break off. Then was the time to think of getting new ones. The entire tribe was in the Black Hills, where they could get all the poles they wanted. They used fir pines, as they were the straightest and could be found in all sizes. The men would chop down as many trees as they needed and haul them to camp one at a time....

[After] all the poles, sticks, pins, and stakes were prepared for the new tepee, the next and hardest job was to get the [buffalo] skins with which to cover the tepee poles. The entire tribe started to move to northern Nebraska, as they knew this to be a good hunting ground. Scouts were sent out ahead to locate the buffalo herds. When they returned with the location of a herd, the hunters would prepare to start out on the hunt.

All the relatives now assembled and entered into an agreement that all the skins from the first hunt were to go to the head of the band. If they did not secure enough hides from the first hunt, then the next one was also to go to him. The hunters would kill as many buffalo as possible, and the skins were removed very carefully. As they were to be used for tepee coverings, there must be no holes in them.

As soon as the hides were brought in, the women spread them on the ground and pegged them out while they were yet fresh, with the flesh side up. Three or four women would then commence to remove all extra bits of meat from the hide. In this work they used a piece of flint or a sharp stone before steel and iron came into use among them. These "fleshers" were shaped like a crowbar with teeth in the end. The handle was covered with buckskin, with a buckskin string attached to tie up around the wrist. [The string] helped to hold the instrument.

After all the meat was removed from the skin and the skin had dried out, it was turned over with the hair on top. Then, with a tool made of elk horn, they scraped off all the hair. This instrument, clasped in both hands, was used by the women, who worked it toward them....

When the hair had all been scraped off, it showed a layer of skin which was dark. This was also removed, showing another layer of white [skin]. This the women took off carefully in little flakes, and it was used in making a very fine soup. The brains and liver of the buffalo were cooked together, after which this mixture was rubbed all over the skin. It was then folded into a square bundle for four or five days. Several of these bundles of skins would be piled on top of each other.

A frame was now built on which to stretch the skin after it was opened. This frame was made of round poles tied together at the four corners with rawhide thongs. When the skin was opened, it was damp. It was fastened to the frame with rawhide rope run through the peg holes around the edge of the hide. The mixture of brain and liver was now all scraped off, and the skin washed with water until perfectly clean. The women then went all over the skin with a sandstone, which made the hide very soft.

A braided sinew was then tied to a naturally bent tree, and the other end was fastened to a stake driven into the ground. This made the sinew taut, like a bowstring. The skin was then taken off the frame and pulled back and forth on this sinew by the women until it was very soft. The effect of this was to produce a beautiful white tan (leather).... When a sufficient number of skins for one tepee was finished, that part of the skin [that had been fastened with peg holes] was trimmed off and the hides were patched together....

In 1850 about twenty million buffalo roamed the Plains. As white settlers moved westward, hunters killed the animals by the thousands. Nowadays about 15,000 buffalo live on fenced game preserves in the United States. In addition, some ranchers raise buffalo for their meat.

When the new tepee was all ready to be put up, the old one was taken down, but the skin covering was not thrown away. Every bit of it was utilized to some good purpose. It was well-smoked, and that made it waterproof. All the long winter, leggings and moccasins were made from the smoked skin. Sometimes a quiver was made to hold the bow and arrows. Later, when the Indians began to get guns, they also made cases for them out of the old hide, so that it was all utilized.

We did not have many cooking utensils. When a buffalo was killed, the men were very careful in removing the stomach so as not to puncture it. The inside lining (or tripe) was washed and hung up on four sticks. This made a sort of bag suspended from the center of the sticks. All the meat was then washed and placed in the stomach-bag. Water and salt were added. Stones were then heated in a fire nearby and put into this bag. The hot stones soon made the water boil, the meat was cooked, and presently we had soup all ready. We then sat down to a feast.

For plates we used the backs of turtles, while some were made from sections cut from trunks of trees and hollowed out. Spoons were made from the horn of the buffalo and the mountain goat. These horns were boiled until soft and then cut down the center. While they were yet hot, the men

The tepees of a Sioux camp dot the wide, open plains.

fashioned them into spoons. Some of these horns were larger than others, and from those was made a sort of dipper.

After all the soup and meat was cleaned out of the [tripe], it was then cut up and eaten. This was a great saving in dishwashing, as there were no pots to wash and our dishes were very few. At that time, we knew nothing of coffee or bread. Our entire bill of fare consisted of meat and soup....

If a change in the bill of fare was desired, the women pounded some dried roasted meat until it was soft and tender. It was then served with the grease from the cooked bones....

In the early spring, when we moved away from our winter quarters, our band of Indians looked better than any circus parade. Each family had its place in line. Nobody was ever in a hurry to get ahead of those in advance....In spite of the fact that there were several hundred people, there was no confusion, no rushing hither and thither, no swearing and no "bossing." Everyone knew we were moving camp, and each did his or her duty without orders. The entire camp would be on the road without any noise.

The old men of the tribe would start out first on foot. They were always in front, and we depended on them. They were experienced and knew the lay of the land perfectly. If the start was made before sunrise, it was beautiful to see the golden glow of the coming day. Then the old men sat down to wait for the sunrise, while the rest of us stood about, holding our horses. One of the men would light the pipe, and, as the sun came over the horizon, the entire tribe stood still as the ceremony to the Great Spirit began. It was a solemn occasion, as the old man held the bowl of the pipe in both hands and pointed the stem toward the sky, then toward the east, south, west, and north, and lastly, to Mother Earth. An appeal was made during this

The Plains Indians made their clothes, tools, and weapons from materials found in their environment, including trees, rocks, and animals.

ceremony. The men smoked, after which the pipe was put away. Sometimes there would be something to eat on these occasions. After this ceremony was over, somehow we felt safer to go on....

We were on our way to our summer home in the northern part of Nebraska, and the distance was considerable....But finally we reached our destination, and our camp was soon settled. Then a scout was picked to go out for buffalo. When the scout returned, the hunters started out. Camp was moved near to the place where the buffalo had been located, so the work would not be so hard on the women by being a great distance from camp. When the fresh meat was brought in, we all had a big feast and were well pleased and satisfied to go to sleep at the end of another day.

Soon the hot summer days arrived....During the heated portion of the day, our parents all sat around in the shade, the women making moccasins, leggings, and other wearing apparel, while the men were engaged in making rawhide ropes for their horses and saddles. Some made hunting arrows, while others made shields and warbonnets....

We children ran around and played, having all the fun we could. In the cool of the evening, after the meal was over, all the big people sat outside, leaning against the tepees. Sometimes there would be footraces or pony races or a ball game. There was plenty we could do for entertainment. Perhaps two or three of the young men who had been on the warpath would dress up in their best clothes, fixing up their best horses with Indian perfume, tie eagle feathers to the animals' tails and on their own foreheads. When they were all set to show off, they would parade around the camp in front of each tepee—especially where there were pretty girls.

We smaller children sat around and watched them. I recall how I wished that I was big enough so I could ride a perfumed horse, all fixed up, and go to see a pretty girl. But I knew that was impossible until I had been on the warpath, and I was too young for that. Before we could turn our thoughts toward such things, we must first know how to fish, kill game, and skin it, how to butcher and bring the meat home, how to handle our horses properly...

When the shades of night fell, we went to sleep, unless our parents decided to have a game of night ball. If they did, then we little folks tried to remain awake to watch the fun. We were never told that we must go to bed because we never objected or cried about getting up in the morning. When we grew tired of playing, we went to our nearest relatives and stayed at their tepee for the night and next morning went home....

Social Customs

The Lakota (Sioux) were a social people, loving human companionship and association and admiring the use of manners and deportment that accompanied their social life.

The rules of polite behavior that formed Lakota etiquette were called *woyuonihan*, meaning "full of respect." Those failing to practice these rules were *waohola sni*, that is, "without respect," therefore rude and ill-bred.

A good deal of time was spent in merrymaking with feasts, songs, dances, and social ceremonies, and anyone coming as a visitor, whether friend or stranger, was welcomed.... The tepee door was always open for anyone to enter, and it was not impolite to walk in without knocking and unannounced. The phrase "come in" was never used to bid one to enter, though when the visitor was in he was at once seated as a mark of hospitality. A stranger, however, coming into the village, especially at night, would call out the fact that he was a stranger and would state his business. The man of the tepee would meet the traveler and on finding him an acceptable visitor would say, "I'll ask my wife to cook you some food." The stranger then followed his host into the tepee, knowing that he would be received as a guest.

When the visitor departed, there were no effusive good-byes and no urgent invitations regarding return visits on either side. The visitor, when ready to leave, would simply say, "It is now time for me to go," and, having so spoken, it would have been poor etiquette to beg him to stay longer.

Praise, flattery, exaggerated manners, and fine, high-sounding words were no part of Lakota politeness. Excessive manners were put down as insincere, and the constant talker was considered rude and thoughtless. Conversation was never begun at once, nor in a hurried manner. No one was quick with a question, no matter how important, and no one was pressed for an answer. A pause giving time for thought was the truly courteous way of beginning and conducting a conversation. Silence was meaningful with the Lakota...[who were] regardful of the rule that "thought comes before speech."

Also in the midst of sorrow, sickness, death, or misfortune of any kind, and in the presence of the notable and great, silence was the mark of respect. More powerful than words was silence with the Lakota and his strict observance of this...good behavior was the reason, no doubt, for his being given another fallacious (false) characterization by the white man—that of being a stoic. He has been adjudged dumb, stupid, indifferent, and unfeeling. As a matter of truth, [a Lakota] was the most sympathetic of men, but his emotions of depth and sincerity were tempered with control...for the silent man was ever to be trusted, while the man ever ready with speech was never taken seriously.

Children were taught the rules of *woyuonihan* and that true politeness was to be defined in actions rather than in words. They were never allowed to pass between the fire and an older person or a visitor, to speak while others were speaking, or to make fun of a crippled or disfigured one. If a child thoughtlessly tried to do so, a parent, in a quiet voice, immediately set [the child] straight. Expressions such as "excuse me," "do pardon me," and "so sorry," now so often lightly and unnecessarily used, are not in the Lakota language. If one chanced to injure or discommode (inconvenience) another, the word *wanunhecun*, or "mistake," was spoken. This was sufficient to indicate that no discourtesy was intended and that an untoward happening was accidental.

Young Indian folk, raised under the old courtesy rules, never indulged in the present habit of talking...all at the same time. To do so would have been not only impolite but foolish, for poise, so much admired as a social grace, could not be accompanied by restlessness. Pauses were acknowledged gracefully and did not cause lack of ease or embarrassment.

A woman of correct social manner was modest, low voiced, and reserved. She sat quietly on the tepee floor, never flouncing herself about nor talking loudly and harshly. A woman who laughed loudly in order to attract attention was put down as common and immoral and was at once discredited and shunned....

A Sioux woman watches over a small child.

Mothers watched over their boys and girls with equal care, though the girls were subjected to more restraint than the boys. [The girls] were given more attention as to personal appearance and were never allowed to sit in a careless way. A girl was instructed to sit properly with her feet to one side and her dress neatly arranged. Never must a young woman sit with her feet and legs out in front of her. In arising she must do so lightly and gracefully, as if without effort, and never lift herself up with both hands. Her movements in the tepee must be noiseless and orderly. The well-bred girl, like her mother, was quiet and modest, and very respectful in the presence of elders. [A] woman's sphere was quite distinctly defined and to obtrude (move away) from it was considered bold and improper...

Men, in the presence of women, were very deferent (respectful)....The taboos of speaking directly to sisters and cousins were strictly observed.... One unacquainted with the rules of polite conduct would be led to think the men cold and indifferent toward their women, though actually their attitude and intent were of extreme respect. I remember, though I was just a small boy, the meeting of my uncle, Brave Eagle, with his love. One night the braves were having a Victory Dance. A beautiful young girl in an elk-tooth-trimmed dress rode up on a handsome spotted pony decorated with a quilled and fringed blanket that covered [the animal] to the heels. This young woman soon had the admiring eyes of all the young braves, and Uncle Brave Eagle was among the many who were smitten with her charms. Though already dressed in his regalia, my uncle went home to put on more finery and to repaint his face. He then picked out his best horse and came back to the dance to wait until the people had begun to disperse. Watching his chance, he joined the young lady and her woman companion as they rode home. Thus began a courtship that ended in the marriage of Brave Eagle and this beautiful young woman....

Only occasionally did a man or woman elect to remain single throughout life, but if he or she did, it was considered a personal affair, and a woman had to be neither a wife nor a mother in order to maintain a place of respect with her people. Elk Woman, I remember, had many suitors, for she was a woman of beauty and the possessor of many virtues, besides being pleasant in manner. But she caused much wonderment, for she turned all away. Finally, Hawk Man, honored in the tribe, came wooing, and their courtship lasted throughout their lives. Though Hawk Man was ever attentive, the two lived with their respective families, and the match considered so ideal by everyone never occurred.

Indian Wisdom

The Lakota was a true…lover of Nature. He loved the earth and all things of the earth, and the attachment grew with age. The old people came literally to love the soil, and they sat or reclined on the ground with a feeling of being close to a mothering power. It was good for the skin to touch the earth, and the old people liked to remove their moccasins and walk with bare feet on the sacred earth. Their tepees were built upon the earth, and their altars were made of earth. The birds that flew in the air came to rest upon the earth, and it was the final resting place of all things that lived and grew. The soil was soothing, strengthening, cleansing, and healing.

This is why the old Indian still sits upon the earth instead of propping himself up and away from its life-giving forces. For him, to sit or lie upon the ground is to be able to think more deeply and to feel more keenly. He can see more clearly into the mysteries of life and come closer in kinship to other lives about him.

The earth was full of sounds which the old-time Indian could hear, sometimes putting his ear to [the ground] so as to hear more clearly. The forefathers of the Lakota had done this for long ages until there had come to them real understanding of earth ways. It was almost as if the man were still a part of the earth as he was in the beginning, according to the legend of the tribe. This beautiful story of the genesis (beginning) of the Lakota people furnished the foundation for the love they bore for earth and all things of the earth. Wherever the Lakota went, he was with Mother Earth. No matter where he roamed by day or slept by night, he was safe with her. This thought comforted and sustained the Lakota, and he was eternally filled with gratitude.

From Wakan Tanka[2] there came a great unifying life force that flowed in and through all things—the flowers of the plains, blowing winds, rocks,

An Indian chants to the Spirits, which the Sioux believed to be present in nature.

The Sioux had great respect for all living things and killed animals only if they were needed for food or clothing.

trees, birds, animals—and was the same force that had been breathed into the first man. Thus all things were kindred and brought together by the same Great Mystery.

Kinship with all creatures of the earth, sky, and water was a real and active principle. For the animal and bird world there existed a brotherly feeling that kept the Lakota safe among them. And so close did some of the Lakota come to their feathered and furred friends that in true brotherhood they spoke a common tongue.

The animal had rights—the right of man's protection, the right to live, the right to multiply, the right to freedom, and the right to man's indebtedness. And in recognition of these rights, the Lakota never captured animals and spared all life that was not needed for food and clothing.

This concept of life and its relations was humanizing and gave to the Lakota an abiding love. It filled his being with the joy and mystery of living. It gave him reverence for all life. It made a place for all things in the scheme of existence with equal importance to all. The Lakota could despise no creature, for all were of one blood, made by the same hand, and filled with the essence of the Great Mystery.

Reflection upon life and its meaning, consideration of its wonders, and observation of the world of creatures began with childhood. The earth, which was called *Maka*, and the sun, called *Anpetuwi*, represented two functions somewhat [like] those of male and female. The earth brought forth life, but the warming, enticing rays of the sun coaxed it into being....

In talking to children, the old Lakota would place a hand on the ground and explain, "We sit in the lap of our Mother. From her we, and all other living things, come. We shall soon pass, but the place where we now rest will last forever." So we, too, learned to sit or lie down on the ground and become conscious of life around us....Sometimes we boys would sit motionless and watch the swallow, the tiny ants, or perhaps some small animal at its work and ponder on its industry and ingenuity. Or we would lay on our backs...and when the stars came out we would make shapes from the various groups. The morning and evening star always attracted attention, and the Milky Way was a path which was traveled by the ghosts.

The old people told us to heed *wa maka skan*, which were the "moving things of earth." This meant, of course, the animals that lived and moved

To the Sioux, lightning and other weather forces displayed special powers.

about, and the stories they told of wa maka skan increased our interest and delight. The wolf, duck, eagle, hawk, spider, bear, and other creatures had marvelous powers, and each one was useful and helpful to us.

Then there were the warriors who lived in the sky and dashed about on their spirited horses during a thunderstorm, their lances clashing with the thunder and glittering with the lightning.... Everything possessed a personality, only differing from us in form.

Knowledge was part of all things. The world was a library, and its books were the stones, leaves, grass, brooks, and the birds and animals that shared with us the storms and blessings of earth. We learned to do what only the student of nature ever learns and that was to feel beauty. We never railed at the storms, the furious winds, and the biting frosts and snows. To do

so intensified human futility, so [we adjusted to whatever came], by more effort and energy if necessary but without complaint. Even the lightning did us no harm, for whenever it came too close, mothers and grandmothers in every tepee put cedar leaves on the coals, and their magic kept danger away. Bright days and dark days were both expressions of the Great Mystery, and the Indian reveled in being close to the Big Holy....

Observation was certain to bring its rewards. Interest, wonder, and admiration grew, and we appreciated the fact that life was more than mere human manifestation—that it was expressed in a multitude of forms. This appreciation enriched Lakota existence. Life was vivid and pulsing. Nothing was casual and commonplace. The Indian lived—lived in every sense of the word—from his first to his last breath.

The character of the Indian's emotion left little room in his heart for antagonism toward his fellow creatures.... For the Lakota, mountains, lakes, rivers, springs, valleys, and woods were all finished beauty. Winds, rain, snow, sunshine, day, night, and change of seasons brought interest. Birds, insects, and animals filled the world with knowledge that defied the understanding of man.

But nothing the Great Mystery placed in the land of the Indian pleased the white man, and nothing escaped his transforming hand. Wherever forests have not been mowed down, wherever the animal is..., wherever the earth is not [lacking] four-footed life—that to him is an "unbroken wilderness." But since for the Lakota there was no wilderness, since nature was not dangerous but hospitable, not forbidding but friendly, Lakota philosophy was healthy—free from fear and dogmatism (biased views). And here I find the great distinction between the faith of the Indian and that of the white man.

Indian faith sought the harmony of man with his surroundings. The [white people] sought the dominance of surroundings. In sharing, in loving all and everything, [the Lakota] naturally found a measure of the thing they sought. While, in fearing, the [white people] found need for conquest. For one man the world was full of beauty. For the other it was a place of sin and ugliness to be endured until he went to another world....

But the old Lakota was wise. He knew that man's heart, away from nature, becomes hard. He knew that lack of respect for growing, living things soon led to a lack of respect for humans, too. So he kept his youth close to [nature's] softening influence.

Religion

The Lakota loved the sun and earth, but he worshiped only Wakan Tanka, or Big Holy (also called the Great Mystery), who was the Maker of all things of earth, sky, and water. Wakan Tanka breathed life and motion into all things, both visible and invisible. He was over all, through all, and in all, and great as was the sun, and good as was the earth. The greatness and goodness of the Big Holy were not surpassed. The Lakota could look at nothing without the same thing looking at Wakan Tanka, and the Lakota could not, if he wished, evade the Big Holy's presence, for it pervaded all things and filled all space. All the mysteries of birth, life, and death and all the wonders of lightning, thunder, wind, and rain were but the evidence of Wakan Tanka's everlasting and encompassing power.

Wakan Tanka prepared the earth and put upon it both man and animal. He dispensed earthly blessings, and, when life on earth was finished, provided...*Wanagi yata*, the place where souls gather. To this home all souls went after death, for there were no wicked to be excluded.

Chapter 5

William Whipple Warren

Ojibway and Chippewa are the common names for the Indian tribe that inhabited the Great Lakes region. But the tribe's traditional name is Anishinabe, meaning "first people." The western division of this tribe settled in northeastern Minnesota—just east of the Great Plains—on lands covered with rich forests and clear lakes. Because of their location near the plains, they became known as the Plains Ojibway.

Some Plains Ojibway lived in permanent settlements and grew corn, beans, squash, and pumpkins in the fertile Minnesota soil. Hunters combed the woodlands for deer, rabbits, and other animals, and fishers plied the deep rivers and lakes. Along the edges of lakes, streams, and swamps, the Ojibway Indians harvested one of their staple foods—wild rice.

The Ojibway author William Whipple Warren was a distinguished historian. Born in Wisconsin in 1825, he later moved to Minnesota, where his fluency in the Ojibway language helped him become an interpreter between the U.S. government and the Ojibway people. In 1850 Warren was elected to the Minnesota Territorial Legislature, where he worked to defend the rights of his people.

Throughout his life, he collected the lore of the Ojibway, compiling this knowledge in History of the Ojibway Nation. His book chronicles the migrations, culture, and folkways of the Anishinabe from early times through the early 1800s.

In northeastern Minnesota, the home of the Ojibway Indians, a roaring waterfall rushes between thick stands of trees.

Selections from
History of the Ojibway Nation

Hunting, Recreation, and Ritual

The Ojibway reside almost exclusively in a wooded country. Their lands are covered with deep and interminable forests, abounding in beautiful lakes and murmuring streams, whose banks are edged with trees of the sweet maple, the useful birch, the tall pine, fir, balsam, cedar, spruce, tamarac, poplar, oak, ash, elm, basswood....

Their country is so interspersed with watercourses that they travel about, up and down streams, from lake to lake, and along the shores of Lake Superior in their light and ingeniously made **birchbark canoes.** From birch-bark and rushes are made the light covering of their simple **wigwams.**

The bands who live on the extreme western borders of their country reside on the borders of the vast western prairies, into which they have gradually driven the fierce Dakota. The Red Lake and Pembina bands, and also the Pillagers, hunt buffalo and other game on the prairies west of the Red River (on the Minnesota-North Dakota border). Thus, as it were, they stood with one foot on the deep eastern forests and the other on the broad western prairies.

The Ojibway, with the exception of a few Lake Superior and Canada bands, live still in their primitive hunter state....They procure food principally by fishing, also by gathering wild rice, hunting deer, and, in some bands, partially by agriculture.

As beaver and the larger animals, such as buffalo, elk, deer, and bear, decreased in number in the immediate vicinity of Leech and Sandy Lakes (in north central Minnesota), the hardy bands of Ojibway who had taken possession of these beautiful sheets of water were obliged to search further into the surrounding country for the game which formed the staple of life. It became customary for these two pioneer bands to meet by appointment every fall of the year at Gull Lake, or at the confluence of the Crow Wing with the Mississippi. From thence [the bands moved] in one collected camp into the more plentifully supplied hunting grounds of the Dakota.

The camp, consisting of between 50 and 100 light birchbark wigwams, moved by short stages from spot to spot, according to the pleasure of the chiefs, or as game was found....This mode of hunting was kept up from the first fall of snow...to the month of February, when the bands again separated, and moved back slowly to their respective village sites, to busy themselves with the manufacture of sugar, amidst the thick groves of... maple...skirting their lakes. As a general fact, only the women occupied themselves in the sugar bushes, while the men scattered about in small bands to hunt the furred animals whose pelts at this season of the year were considered to be most valuable.

When sugar making was over and the ice and snow had once more disappeared before the warmth of a spring sun, the scattered wigwams of the different bands would once more collect at their village sites, and the time for recreation, ball-playing, racing, courtship, and war had once more arrived. If no trader had passed the winter amongst them, many of the hunters would start off in their birch canoes to visit the trading posts on the Great Lakes, to barter their pelts for new supplies of clothing, ammunition, tobacco, and firewater (liquor).

In winter, when lakes and rivers froze, the Ojibway played games on the slick ice.

The Ojibway collected sap from maple trees and boiled the liquid until it turned into syrup. They then let the syrup harden into cakes of maple sugar.

If anyone had lately lost relatives, naturally or at the hands of the Dakota, now was the proper time to think of revenge. It is generally at this season of the year that war parties…prowled all over the northwestern country.…

The spring of the year is also the favorite time for the performance of [the rites of] the sacred grand Meda-we (a secret society whose members have a link to the spirit world). The person wishing to become an initiate into the secrets of this religion, which the old men affirm [is a gift from] the Great Spirit…prepares himself during the whole winter for the approaching ceremony. He collects and dries choice meats. With the choicest pelts, he procures…articles for sacrifice. When spring arrives, having chosen

Working from birchbark canoes, Ojibway Indians harvest wild rice, which grows in shallow lakes.

his four initiators (sponsors) from the wise old men of his village, he places these articles, with tobacco, at their disposal, and the ceremonies commence. For four nights, the medicine drums of the initiators resound throughout the village, and their songs and prayers are addressed to the master of life. The day that the ceremony is performed is one of jubilee to the inhabitants of the village. Each [person] dons the best clothing he or she possesses. They vie with one another in the paints and ornaments... they [wear] to appear to the best advantage within the sacred lodge.

It is at this season of the year also, in which…the young men amuse themselves in playing their favorite…game[s]….During this season, the women generally spend time making their lodge coverings and mats for use during the coming winter and picking and drying berries. Their hard work, however, again commences in the autumn, when the wild rice, which abounds in many of the northern inland lakes, becomes ripe and fit to gather. Then, for a month or more, they are busied in laying in their winter's supply.

When the rice gathering is over, the autumn is far advanced….[After] each family has secreted (stored) their rice and other property with which they do not wish to be encumbered during the coming winter's march, they move once more in a body to the usual rendezvous at Gull Lake or at Crow Wing. [They] search for meat on the dangerous hunting grounds of their enemies. In those days of which we now speak, game of the larger species was very plentiful in this region of country, where now a poor Ojibway depending on his hunt for a living would literally starve to death.

Chapter 6

Waheenee

In 1804 the U.S. explorers Meriwether Lewis and William Clark visited the fortified Villages of the Willows, a settlement of the Hidatsa on the Upper Missouri River. There, in what are now the plains of North Dakota, the Hidatsa lived in relative peace and harmony alongside their allies, the Mandan.

Hidatsa hunters trailed the buffalo, using the meat to supplement their crops. Some tribal members stayed behind during the hunt, planting pumpkins, peas, corn, and squash. Because the Hidatsa lived in permanent villages located near their fields, their daily lives were more stable than those of the tribes who followed the hunt. Tribal members had time for recreation and for crafts, including pottery, beadwork, and hide painting.

During the winter of 1837 and 1838, disaster struck the Hidatsa. White people passing through the area carried smallpox, a deadly disease unknown to the tribe before that time. This epidemic, along with an outbreak of measles and cholera, wiped out nearly all the Hidatsa and the Mandan.

Three years later, a Hidatsa girl was born at Fort Berthold, a reservation in North Dakota where many of the survivors lived. She was named Waheenee-wea, meaning "Buffalo-Bird Woman." Like other Hidatsa girls, she performed difficult tasks at an early age and quickly learned her role in community life. In her later years, she served as a tribal historian.

From 1908 to 1918, Waheenee dictated stories of her youth, marriage, and child-rearing experiences to Gilbert L. Wilson. Her son, Edward Goodbird, translated and illustrated Waheenee: An Indian Girl's Story, which offers a close look at nineteenth-century tribal life and at the heart and mind of a Hidatsa woman.

A river winds between low bluffs in western North Dakota.

Selections from
Waheenee:
An Indian Girl's Story

Childhood

I was born in an earth lodge by the mouth of the Knife River, in what is now North Dakota, three years after the smallpox winter. The Mandan and my tribe, the Hidatsa, had come years before from the Heart River, and they had built the Five Villages, as we called them, on the banks of the Knife, near the place where it enters the Missouri [River].

Here were bottomlands for our cornfields and cottonwood trees for the beams and posts of our lodges. The dead wood that floated down either river would help keep us in firewood, the old women thought. Getting fuel in a prairie country was not always easy work.

When I was ten days old, my mother made a feast and asked an old man named Nothing But Water to give me a name. He called me Good Way. "For I pray the gods," he said, "that our little girl may go through life by a good way, that she may grow up a good woman, not quarreling nor stealing, and that she may have good luck all her days."

I was a rather sickly child, and my father, Small Ankle, wished after a time to give me a new name. We thought that sickness was from the gods. A child's name was given him as a kind of prayer. A new name, our medicine men thought, often moved the gods to help a sick or weakly child.

So my father gave me another name, Waheenee-wea, or Buffalo-Bird Woman. In our Hidatsa language, *waheenee* means cowbird or buffalo-bird, as this little brown bird is known in the buffalo country. *Wea*, meaning girl or woman, is often added to a girl's name so that no one mistakes it for the name of a boy. I do not know why my father chose this name. His gods, I know, were birds, and these, we thought, had much holy power. Perhaps the buffalo-birds had spoken to him in a dream.

I am still called by the name my father gave me. As I have lived to be a very old woman, I think it has brought me good luck from the gods.

My mother's name was Weahtee. She was one of four sisters, all wives of my father. Her sisters' names were Red Blossom, Stalk of Corn, and Strikes Many Woman. I was taught to call all these my mothers. Such was our Indian custom. I do not think my mother's sisters could have been kinder to me if I had been [their] own daughter.

I remember nothing of our life at the Five Villages, but my great-grandmother, White Corn, told me something of it. I used to creep into her bed when the nights were cold and beg for stories.

"The Mandan lived in two of the villages, the Hidatsa in three," she said. "Around each village, except on the side that fronted the river, ran a fence of posts with spaces between for shooting arrows. In front of the row of posts was a deep ditch.

"We had corn aplenty and buffalo meat to eat in the Five Villages, and there were old people and little children in every lodge. Then smallpox came. More than half of my tribe died in the smallpox winter. Of the Mandan, only a few families were left alive. All the old people and little children died."

I was sad when I heard this story. "Did any of your family die, Great-Grandmother?" I asked.

"Yes, my husband, Yellow Elk, died. So many were the dead that there was no time to put up burial scaffolds. So his clan fathers bore Yellow Elk to the burying ground and laid him on the grass with logs over him to keep off the wolves...."

Enemies gave our tribes much trouble after the smallpox year, my grandmother said. Bands of Sioux waylaid hunting parties or came prowling around our villages to steal horses. Our chiefs, both Mandan and Hidatsa, held a council and decided to move farther up the Missouri. "We will build a new village," they agreed, "and dwell together as one tribe."

The site chosen for the new village was a place called Like a Fishhook Point, a bit of high benchland that jutted into a bend of the Missouri. We set out for our new home in the spring, when I was four years old. I remember nothing of our march.... My mothers have told me that not many horses were then owned by the Hidatsa, and that robes, pots, axes, bags of corn, and other stuff were packed on the backs of women or on **travois** dragged by dogs.

The march was led by the older chiefs and medicine men. My grandfather was one of them. His name was Missouri River. On the pommel of his saddle hung his medicines or sacred objects—two human skulls wrapped in a skin. They were believed to be the skulls of Thunderbirds, who, before they died, had changed themselves into Indians. After the chiefs, in a long line, came warriors, women, and children. Young men who owned ponies

When they moved camp, many Plains groups packed their belongings in travois (sleds), which were dragged by dogs or horses.

were sent ahead to hunt meat for the evening camp. Others rode up and down the line to speed the stragglers and to see that no child strayed off to fall into the hands of our enemies, the Sioux.

The earth lodges that the Mandan and Hidatsa built were dome-shaped houses of posts and beams roofed over with willows and grass and earth. But every family owned a tepee, or skin tent, for use when hunting or traveling. Our two tribes camped in those tents the first summer at Like a Fishhook Point and cleared ground for cornfields.

The labor of clearing was done chiefly by the women, although the older men helped. Young men were expected to be off fighting our enemies or

In this drawing by a Hidatsa artist, a hunter on horseback prepares to shoot a buffalo with his bow and arrow.

hunting buffalo. There was need for hunting. Our small first year's fields could yield no large crops, and, to keep from going hungry in the winter months, we had to lay in a good store of dried meat. We owned few guns in the tribe then, and hunting buffalo with arrows was anything but sport. Only young men, strong and active, made good hunters.

My mothers were hard-working women and began their labor of clearing a field almost as soon as camp was pitched. My grandmother, Turtle, chose the ground for the field. It was in a piece of bottomland that lay along the river, a little east of the camp. My mothers had brought seed corn from the Five Villages, as well as squash, bean, and sunflower seed.

I am not sure that they were able to plant much corn the first season. I know they planted some beans and a few squashes. I am told that when the squash harvest came in, my grandmother picked out a long green-striped squash for me, for a doll baby. I carried this about on my back, snuggled under my buffalo-calf robe, as I had seen Indian mothers carry their babies. At evening, I wrapped my dolly in a bit of skin and put her to bed.

Our camp on a summer's evening was a cheerful scene. At this hour, fires burned before most of the tepees and, as the women had ended their day's labors, there was much visiting from tent to tent. Here a family sat eating their evening meal. Yonder, a circle of old men, cross-legged or squat-on-heels in the firelight, joked and told stories. From a big tent on one side of the camp came the tum-tum tum-tum of a drum. We had dancing almost every evening in those good days.

But for wee folks bedtime was rather early. In my father's family, it was soon after sunset. My mothers had laid dry grass around the tent wall, and on this had spread buffalo skins for beds. Small logs laid along the edge of the beds caught any sparks from the fireplace. For, when the nights grew

Two women pull their boats ashore near a Mandan village, which is perched on a bluff overlooking the Missouri River in North Dakota.

Many women of the Plains wore robes that were made of animal hide and decorated with colorful geometric designs.

chilly, my mothers made their fire in the tepee. My father often sat and sang me to sleep by the firelight.

Learning to Work

My mothers began to teach me household tasks when I was about twelve years old. "You are getting to be a big girl," they said. "Soon you will be a woman and marry. Unless you learn to work, how will you feed your family?"

One of the things given me to do was fetching water from the river. No spring was near our village and, anyhow, our prairie springs are often bitter with alkali (a salt present in some soils). But the Missouri River, fed by melting snows of the Montana mountains, gave us plenty of fresh water. Missouri River water is muddy, but it soon settles and is cool and sweet to drink. We Indians love our big river, and we are glad to drink of its waters, as drank our fathers.

A steep path led down the bank to the watering place. Down this path, the village girls made their way every morning to get water for drinking and cooking. They went in little groups or in pairs. Two girls, cousins or chums, sometimes swung a freshly filled pail from a pole on their shoulders....

We girls liked to go to the watering place. For, while we were filling our buckets, we could gossip with our friends. For older girls and young men it was a place for courtship. A youth, with painted face and trailing hair switch (a heavy, thick strand), would loiter near the path, and smile slyly at his sweetheart as she passed. She did not always smile back. Sometimes for long weeks she held her eyes away, not even glancing at his moccasins. It was a shy smile that she gave him at last. Nor did she talk with her love-boy—as we called him—when others were about. We should have thought that silly. But he might wait for her at sunset by her father's lodge and talk with her in the twilight.

But I had other tasks besides fetching water. I learned to cook, sweep, and sew with awl and sinew. Red Blossom taught me to embroider with quills of gull and porcupine dyed in colors. Sometimes I helped at harder work, gathering driftwood at the river, dressing or scraping hides, and even helping in our cornfield.

I liked to go with my mothers to the cornfields in planting time, when the spring sun was shining and the birds were singing in the treetops. How good it seemed to be out under the open sky after the long months in our winter camp! A cottonwood tree stood at a turn of the road to our field. Every season a pair of magpies built their nest in it. They were saucy birds and scolded us roundly when we passed. How I used to laugh at their wicked scoldings!

I am afraid I did not help my mothers much. Like any young girl, I liked better to watch the birds than to work. Sometimes I chased away the crows. Our corn indeed had many enemies, and we had to watch that they did not get our crop. Magpies and crows destroyed much of the young corn. Crows were fond of pulling up the [young] plants.... Spotted gophers dug up the roots of the young corn to nibble the soft seed.

When our field was all planted, Red Blossom used to go back and replant any hills that the birds had destroyed. Where she found a plant missing, she dug a little hole with her hand and dropped in a seed, or I dropped it in for her.

It was hard work, stooping to plant in the hot sun, and Red Blossom never liked having to go over the field a second time. "Those bad crows," she would groan, "they make us much trouble."

My grandmother...made scarecrows to frighten away the birds. In the middle of the field she drove two sticks for legs and bound two other sticks to them for arms. On the top, she fastened a ball of castaway skins for a head. She belted an old robe about the figure to make it look like a man. Such a scarecrow looked wicked! Indeed I was almost afraid of it myself. But the bad crows, seeing that the scarecrow never moved from its place, soon lost their fear and came back.

In the months of midsummer, the crows did not give us much trouble. But as soon as the Moon of Cherries drew near, they became worse than ever. The corn had now begun [to grow in ears], and the crows and blackbirds came in flocks to peck open the green ears for the soft kernels. Many families now built stages in their fields, where the girls and young women

To protect the ripening corn from hungry birds, young Hidatsa girls climbed onto tall platforms, where they sang songs, shook rattles, and flapped blankets to scare away the birds.

To celebrate a crop of new corn, the Hidatsa performed the Green Corn Dance.

of the household came to sit and sing as they watched that crows and other thieves did not steal the ripening grain.

We cared for our corn in those days as we would care for a child. For we Indian people loved our fields as mothers love their children. We thought that the corn plants had souls, as children have souls, and that the growing corn liked to hear us sing, as children like to hear their mother's sing to them. Nor did we want the birds to come and steal our corn after the hard work of planting and hoeing. Horses, too, might break into the field, or boys might steal the green ears and go off and roast them....

Girls began to go on the watchers' stage when they reached about ten or twelve years of age, and many kept up the custom after they were grown

up and married. Older women, working in the field and stopping to rest, often went on the [watchers'] stage and sang.

Marriage

And so I grew up, a happy, contented Indian girl, obedient to my mothers, but loving them dearly. I learned to cook, dress skins, embroider, sew with awl and sinew, and cut and make moccasins, clothing, and tent covers. There was always plenty of work to do, but I had time to rest and to go to see my friends, and I was not given tasks beyond my strength. My father did the heavy lifting, if posts or beams were to be raised. "You are young, daughter," he would say. "Take care you do not overstrain!" He was a kind man and helped my mothers and me whenever we had hard work to do.

For my industry in dressing skins, my clan aunt, Sage, gave me a woman's belt. It was as broad as my three fingers, and covered with blue beads. One end was made long, to hang down before me. Only a very industrious girl was given such a belt. She could not buy or make one....To wear a woman's belt was an honor.

I won other honors by my industry. For embroidering a robe with porcupine quills for my father, I was given a brass ring, bought from the traders.

The inside of a lodge was large enough for a family to live comfortably and to store all its belongings.

And for embroidering a tent cover with gull quills dyed yellow and blue, I was given a bracelet. There were few girls in the village who owned belt, ring, and bracelet.

In these years of my girlhood, my mothers were watchful of all that I did. We had big dances in the village where men and women sang, drums beat loud, and young men, painted and feathered, danced and yelled to show their brave deeds. I did not go to these dances often, and when I did my mothers were very careful of me.

I was eighteen years old the Bent Enemy Killed winter. For we Hidatsa reckoned by winters, naming each for something that happened in it. An old man named Hanging Stone then lived in the village. He had a stepson named Magpie, a handsome young man and a good hunter.

One morning Hanging Stone came into our lodge. It was a little while after our morning meal, and I was putting away the wooden bowls that we used for dishes. The hollow buffalo hoofs hung on the door for bells, I remember, rattled clitter, clitter, clitter, as he raised and let fall the door. My father was sitting by the fire.

Hanging Stone walked up to my father and laid his right hand on my father's head. "I want you to believe what I say," he cried. "I want my boy to live in your good family. I am poor, you are rich, but I want you to favor us and do as I ask."

He went over to my mothers and did likewise, speaking the same words to them. He then strode out of the lodge.

Neither my father nor my mothers said anything, and I did not know at first what it all meant. (Hanging Stone wanted Buffalo-Bird Woman to marry his stepson.) My father sat for a while, looking at the fire. At last he spoke, "My daughter is too young to marry. When she is older I may be willing."

Toward evening Hanging Stone and his relatives brought four horses and three flintlock guns to our lodge. He tied the four horses to the drying stage outside. They had good bridles, with chains hanging to the bits. On the back of each horse was a blanket and some yards of calico, [a] very expensive [cloth] in those days.

Hanging Stone came into the lodge. "I have brought you four horses and three guns," he said to my father.

"I must refuse them," answered Small Ankle. "My daughter is too young to marry."

Hanging Stone went away, but he did not take his horses with him. My father sent them back by some young men.

The evening of the second day after, Hanging Stone came again to our lodge. As before, he brought the three guns and gifts of cloth and four horses. But two of these were hunting horses. A hunting horse was one fleet enough to overtake a buffalo, a thing that few of our little Indian ponies could do. Such horses were costly and hard to get. A family that had good hunting horses had always plenty of meat.

After Hanging Stone left, my father said to his wives, "What do you think about it?"

"We would rather not say anything," they answered. "Do as you think best."

"I know this Magpie," said my father. "He is a kind young man. I have refused his gifts once, but I see his heart is set on having our daughter. I think I shall agree to it."

Turning to me he spoke, "My daughter, I have tried to raise you right. I have hunted and worked hard to give you food to eat. Now I want you to take my advice. Take this man for your husband. Try always to love him. Do not think in your heart, 'I am a handsome young woman, but this man, my husband, is older and not handsome.' Never taunt your husband. Try not to do anything that will make him angry."

I did not answer yes or no to this, for I thought, "If my father wishes me to do this, why that is the best thing for me to do." I had been taught to be obedient to my father. I do not think white children are taught so, as we Indian children were taught.

For nigh a week my father and my mothers were busy getting ready the feast foods for the wedding. On the morning of the sixth day, my father took from his bag a fine weasel-skin cap and an eagle-feather warbonnet. The first he put on my head, the second he handed to my sister, Cold Medicine. "Take these things to Hanging Stone's lodge," he said.

We were now ready to march. I led, my sister walking with me. Behind us came some of our relatives leading three horses. And after them, five great kettles of feast foods on poles borne on the shoulders of women relatives.

White missionaries gather at a sewing meeting with Hidatsa women in 1897, when most Hidatsa were living on a reservation in North Dakota.

The kettles held boiled dried green corn and ripe corn pounded to meal and boiled with beans. And they were steaming hot.

There was a covered entrance to Hanging Stone's lodge. The light was rather dim inside, and I did not see a dog lying there until he sprang up, bark[ed], and dashed past me. I sprang back, startled. Cold Medicine tittered. "Do not be foolish," called one of our women relatives. Cold Medicine stopped her tittering, but I think we were rather glad of the dog. My sister and I had never marched in a wedding before, and we were both a little scared.

I lifted the skin door—it was an old-fashioned one swinging on thongs from the beam overhead—and entered the lodge. Hanging Stone sat on his couch against the...fire screen. I went to him and put the weasel-skin cap on his head. The young man who was to be my husband was [also] sitting on the couch....Cold Medicine and I went over and shyly sat on the floor nearby.

The kettles of feast foods had been set down near the fireplace, and the three horses [had been] tied to the corn stage. Hanging Stone had fetched my father four horses. We reckoned the weasel cap and the warbonnet as worth each a horse and, with these and our three horses, my father felt he was going his friend one horse better. It was a point of honor in an Indian family for the bride's father to make a more valuable return gift than that brought him by the bridegroom and his friends.

We two girls sat on the floor with ankles to the right as Indian women always sit. Magpie's mother filled a wooden bowl with dried buffalo meat pounded fine and mixed with marrow fat and set it for my sister and me to eat. We ate as much as we could. What was left, my sister put in a fold of her robe, and we arose and went home. It would have been impolite to leave behind any of the food given us to eat.

Later in the day, Magpie's relatives and friends came to feast on the foods we had taken to Hanging Stone's lodge. Each guest brought a gift, something useful to a newlywed bride—beaded work, fawn-skin work bag, girl's leggings, belt, blanket, woman's robe, calico for a dress, and the like. In the evening, two women of Magpie's family brought these gifts to my father's lodge, packing them each in a blanket on her back. They piled the gifts on the floor beside Red Blossom, the elder of my mothers.

Red Blossom spent the next few days helping me build and decorate the couch that was to mark off the part of our lodge set apart for my husband and me. We even made and placed before the couch a fine, roomy lazy-back, or willow chair.

All being now ready, Red Blossom said to me, "Go and call your husband. Go and sit beside him and say, 'I want you to come to my father's lodge.' Do not feel shy. Go boldly and have no fear."

So with my sister I slowly walked to Hanging Stone's lodge. There were several [people] besides the family within, for they were expecting me, but no one said anything as we entered.

Magpie was sitting on his couch....My sister and I went over and sat beside him. Magpie smiled and said, "What have you come for?"

"I have come to call you," I answered....

Cold Medicine and I arose and returned to my father's lodge. Magpie followed us a few minutes later, for young men did not walk through the village with their sweethearts in the daytime. We should have thought that foolish. And so I was wed.

After Fifty Years

I am an old woman now. The buffalo and black-tail deer are gone, and our Indian ways are almost gone. Sometimes I find it hard to believe that I ever lived them.

My little son grew up in the white man's school. He can read books, and he owns cattle and has a farm. He is a leader among our Hidatsa people, helping teach them to follow the white man's road. He is kind to me. We no longer live in an earth lodge but in a house with chimneys. And my son's wife cooks by a stove.

But for me, I cannot forget our old ways. Often in summer I rise at daybreak and steal out to the cornfields. And as I hoe the corn I sing to it, as we did when I was young. No one cares for our corn songs now.

Sometimes at evening I sit, looking out on the big Missouri. The sun sets, and dusk steals over the water. In the shadows I seem again to see our Indian village, with smoke curling upward from the earth lodges. And in the river's roar I hear the yells of the warriors, the laughter of little children as of old. It is but an old woman's dream. Again I see but shadows and hear only the roar of the river, and tears come into my eyes. Our Indian life, I know, is gone forever.

Chapter 7

Jim Whitewolf

In the early nineteenth century, an Apache band from the deserts of what is now the southwestern United States settled near the Kiowa people on the southern Great Plains. The Apache group, which closely associated itself with the Kiowa, became known as the Kiowa-Apache.

The Kiowa-Apache eventually became typical Plains dwellers. They traded horses and hunted wild game. Although constantly on the move, the Kiowa-Apache maintained close family ties, with many generations living together in the same household. Elders taught tribal values and religious traditions to the young.

Tribal historian Jim Whitewolf was born in 1878, about a decade after the U.S. government forced the Kiowa-Apache onto the Oklahoma reservation they occupy today. Officials sent Kiowa-Apache youths to government schools, where they were taught to reject their traditional way of life. As a result, many Kiowa-Apache lost their sense of heritage. In addition, they were not taught the skills needed to find work in an increasingly industrialized society, and many ended up without jobs or hope.

As a child, Jim Whitewolf learned the old ways of his people. As an adult, he was out of place in a changing world, and he longed for a return to the old life. Reflecting on his past, Jim Whitewolf dictated his autobiography, Jim Whitewolf: The Life of a Kiowa-Apache Indian. Later edited by Charles Brant, Whitewolf's story illustrates how Kiowa-Apache society changed after the tribe came in contact with white people.

*Mountains loom above the horizon of
Oklahoma's plains.*

Selections from
Jim Whitewolf:
The Life of a
Kiowa-Apache Indian

Early Years

When I was a pretty small boy, my grandmother used to tell me, "Always wear your moccasins when you walk around. Don't run around with your hair blowing everywhere." She braided my hair for me. My mother told her to raise me right and to take care of me.

I had two dogs that I played with. My grandfather fixed a rope for me to lasso the dogs and lead them around by. He made me a set of arrows and a bow. The arrows were blunt ended, and the bow was small, like children used. He told me not to shoot at anything except birds.[1] He told me, "Certain boys go way off when they play. Don't go with them because they are crazy."[2] He said to swim only with boys my own size, because big boys might drown me. I would play around with my bow and arrows until I got tired of [the game]. Then I would rope my dogs and pretend they were horses. When my father went out to round up his horses, I rode with him on the back of the saddle. He showed me how to stop a horse to catch it. I would hold out my hand like I was going to feed the horse, and then it would stop. I learned how to hobble horses, too....[3]

One time my grandfather caught one of his gentlest horses and told me, "Ride him bareback." In the evening, I rode that horse as we took the other horses to be watered. That is how he taught me to ride. When I had learned, he pointed out a certain boy who liked to hunt. He told me, "Go with him to chase rabbits and shoot birds."

One morning my grandfather got me up early and said, "Take your horse. Put the bridle on him and go out and water our horses. Take off the hobbles and put the ropes around their necks. Take them down to the water. You have seen how I do it." I did it myself that time.

As I went around with other boys chasing rabbits and squirrels, some of us got to be pretty good shots with a bow and arrow. Later I was taught to shoot a .44 Winchester. My grandfather took me out by a hill and put down a bone for a target. He showed me how to sight with the rifle. At first I was a little afraid. I didn't shoot very well at the beginning, so the bullets just went off anywhere....By this time I was growing up to be a pretty good-sized boy.

Then my grandfather gave me a rope, a bridle, and a saddle. He said I knew how to handle horses and could go about it myself. The saddle had a case on it for the rifle. Then he gave me the rifle.

Sometime before the country opened up,[4] my grandfather died. They didn't kill his horse at the funeral or anything like that in the old-time way. My father said to me, "Now that your grandfather is gone, some of his horses will be yours. Take care of them as he taught you to." My grandfather, before he died, had told my father which of the horses were to be mine.

I went home to stay with my father and mother then. They made a place for me to sleep. They made me buckskin clothes to wear when I went to the dances. I had a buckskin jacket that went over my head and leggings that fitted tight. My father told me, "You have horses, clothes, saddle, and bridle. You have your own things, so when you get married you are all ready...." My parents said that if you had a good start and were raised right, you would be a well-respected man when you grew up....

That is how they raised you up in the old days. They gave you things and taught you things, and when you were grown they would tell you, "Use these things right. Do not cheat or lie. Treat others right, and do not hurt their feelings." They said that if you did not act right, others would laugh at you, and everything you had would be poor. Then you would be ashamed. They said, "When you get married and have your children, raise them in a religious way." Up to the time I got married, I did the things I was told.

When I was growing up, I saw something of how my grandmother taught my sister. She showed her how to make little tepees out of cloth and how to make little cradles. She told her to keep the little tepees clean. As girls grew older, they were taught to make bigger tepees and how to cook. They would ask for a piece of the meat when the women were cooking and take it to their own fires and put it in a bucket, just like they saw the women do.

When my sister was grown up, my mother's half-sister taught her to do beadwork. My sister watched her and tried to imitate her as she sewed and made baby clothes. Her play days were over now. She watched my mother and learned how to cook and to prepare meals. After she went to school,

Apache women in Arizona weave baskets with geometrical designs. During the 1800s, some Apache migrated eastward to the Plains and joined with the Kiowa. This group came to be known as the Kiowa-Apache.

she began to sew her own clothes at home. When she got married, she had all her own things.

Preparing Food

This is about the food we ate when I was young. They used to slice the meat up thin and hang it up to dry in the sun. That way it would keep for the winter. My mother used to put it into a bag made of hide to keep

By the 1870s, many Kiowa-Apache had been forced to move their camps onto a reservation in Oklahoma.

it. She broke up the bones of the cow and boiled them to get the grease out. She put the grease into a bag [made] of cow udder that had a buckskin drawstring. She didn't like buckets because she thought they would spoil things. The meat from the back of the animal she cooked and dried. It was something like bacon. She took the large intestine and stuffed it with a long piece of raw meat. The whole thing was boiled and eaten.

We gathered wild grapes in the fall. They were boiled up, mixed with a little flour, and made into balls like hamburgers. They put them into a skin bag to keep. There were wild blue grapes with seeds in them. It used to be women's work to gather the grapes, but when I was young, boys did it, too. Wild plums were prepared in the same way.

Mesquite beans were ground up sometimes with rocks and put away. Some people just kept them as they were. They used the ground-up ones like cornmeal.

Hackberries grew on big trees. They were ground up and formed into balls and put away. There was another berry that we call "rock sour." They were dried and kept, too.

When I was a boy, living with my parents, we had dried meat and dried fruit for every meal. We used to have meat soup a lot, too. We ate hard-boiled eggs from wild turkeys and prairie chickens. Whenever we ate fish, they were cooked right in the ashes. Rabbits were roasted that way, too.

My favorite food was ground-up meat with sugar mixed in it. They mixed the meat with marrow [bone tissue] before they sweetened it. All the small children liked this the best. My mother would give it to me all the time. They used the meat from the backbone to make pounded meat for the children. They kept it separate from the other meat. People who had a lot of pounded meat on hand were considered well off. It was kept for times when…fresh meat [was scarce].

My father's sister[5] always treated me good. When I went there, she would feed me well. She would make me a good bed to sleep in, and sometimes she sewed my clothes and shoes. Whenever I went to see my grandmother, she gave my mother dried fruits to give me. My mother's brother's wife[5] would do the same.

When I was a small boy, there were only antelopes, deer, and wild turkeys. I don't remember any buffalo. One time [the men] were gathering together

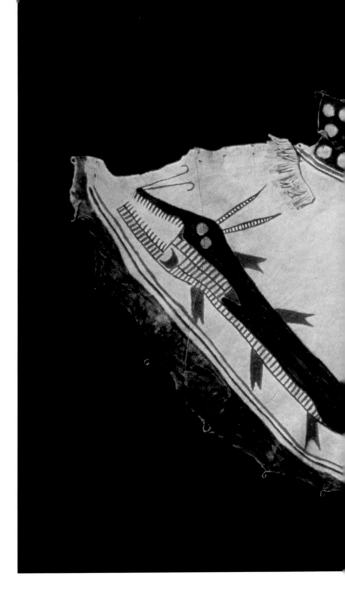

The Kiowa often painted their tepees with colorful decorations, such as these monsters. According to an ancient Kiowa story, the monsters waited underwater to trap swimmers.

to talk about hunting. They wanted only the fastest horses—the ones that knew how to follow the deer. I had a small pony then. Some old Kiowa gave [the animal] to my mother, and she gave it to me. I never had gone out with it chasing deer or antelope. I just went out on the prairies with it to chase coyotes.

That morning...they were going to gather together early....When they got up north of what is now Apache (a city in Oklahoma), they scattered out. Some went up on high ground, and some went down into low places.

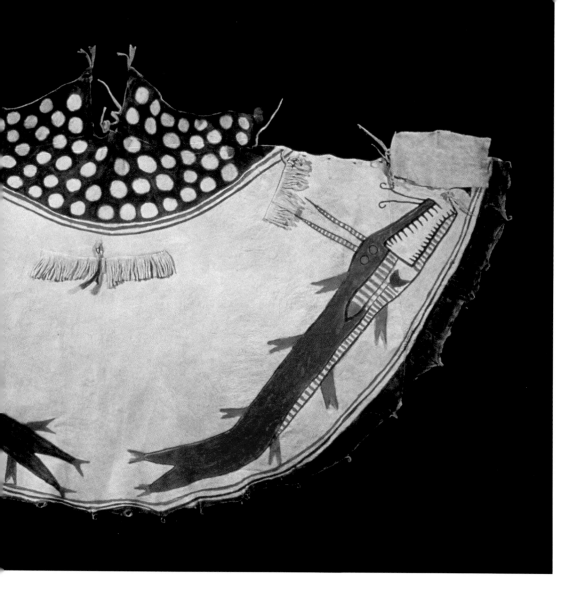

Just east of where I was riding, someone hollered and they began to shoot. Then I saw three deer come out into an open place. The hunters began to chase these deer all around....[But] then the horses got tired and these fellows started to fall back. One deer came rushing toward me, and I ran right into it with my horse, [which] knocked the deer down as I jumped from my horse. I ran over to where the deer was lying and grabbed hold of it. A big fellow rode up and cut the deer's throat with a knife. Then he grabbed a hind leg and said, "This is going to be mine."

An Apache prepares his bow and arrows for hunting.

The others rode up and jumped off their horses. There were six parts of the deer, the four legs and the sides. Each of the six men claimed a part, and I was left with just the backbone and the hide. They washed the kidneys, liver, and the gall (bladder) in blood and ate them right there. They took a piece of the gall and put it on the liver, to give it a salty, bitter taste. When they were through butchering and each had his share, we went back. That was the law about hunting deer—the one that killed it got only the backbone and hide.

On the way back, one of the fellows with a .44 Winchester shot two more deer.... Then two fellows had a race to the deer to claim their parts, the ribs. We went on back to camp. That was the first time I ever went deer hunting.

Chapter 8

Black Elk

Black Elk was a wichasha wakon—a holy man of the Oglala Sioux (Lakota). His life spanned almost a century. Born in 1863 on the Dakota plains, he fought in the wars to save the Black Hills from white invaders. When the wars ended in defeat, the government forced Black Elk and the rest of his tribe onto the Pine Ridge Reservation in western South Dakota, where he lived until his death in 1950.

In 1931 the poet John G. Neihardt persuaded the aging holy man to dictate the story of his life. Neihardt edited the narrative and published it the next year. Entitled Black Elk Speaks, the book tells of the time when the Oglala Sioux traveled freely on the Dakota plains, following the laws and traditions of their ancestors. Black Elk recounts the wars against the invading white people, the destruction of the tribal way of life, and the breakdown of tribal religion.

In the narrative, Black Elk also recalls his efforts to inspire his people to return to the faith of their ancestors. In early Sioux religion, the people respected beauty and truth. If the people returned to their religion, said Black Elk, they would find peace within themselves. Through religion, they could unite and walk together on the "good red road."

The rich colors of a sunset streak across the sky over South Dakota's plains.

Selections from
Black Elk Speaks:
Being the Life Story of a
Holy Man of the Oglala Sioux

A Prophecy Fulfilled

Once we were happy in our own country, and we were seldom hungry, for then the two-leggeds and the four-leggeds lived together like relatives, and there was plenty for them and for us. But the Wasichus (white people) came, and they have made little islands for us and other little islands for the four-leggeds. Always these islands are becoming smaller, for around them surges the gnawing flood of the Wasichu, and it is dirty with lies and greed.

A long time ago, my father told me what his father told him—that there was once a Lakota holy man called Drinks Water who dreamed what was to be. This was long before the coming of the Wasichus. He dreamed that the four-leggeds were going back into the earth and that a strange race had woven a spider's web all around the Lakota. And he said: "When this happens, you shall live in square gray houses, in a barren land, and beside those square gray houses you will starve."

They say he went back to Mother Earth soon after he saw this vision, and it was sorrow that killed him. You can look about you now and see that he meant these dirt-roofed houses we are living in, and that all the rest was true. Sometimes dreams are wiser than waking.

The Sacred Voices

I was four years old, and I think it must have been the next summer that I first heard the voices. It was a happy summer, and no one was afraid, because in the Moon When the Ponies Shed (May) word came from the Wasichus that there would be peace...and that all the soldiers would go away. The soldiers did go away, and their towns were torn down. And in the Moon of Falling Leaves (November), they made a treaty with Red Cloud that said our country would be ours as long as grass should grow and water flow....

Maybe it was not this summer when I first heard the voices, but I think it was, because I know it was before I played with bows and arrows or rode a horse, and I was out playing alone when I heard them. It was like somebody calling me, and I thought it was my mother, but there was nobody there. This happened more than once and always made me afraid so that I ran home.

It was when I was five years old that my grandfather made me a bow and some arrows. The grass was young and I was on horseback. A thunderstorm was coming from where the sun goes down, and just as I was riding into the woods along a creek, there was a kingbird sitting on a limb. This was not a dream, it happened. And I was going to shoot at the kingbird with the bow my grandfather made, when the bird spoke: "The clouds all over are one-sided." Perhaps it meant that all the clouds were looking at me. And then it said, "Listen! A voice is calling you!" Then I looked up at the clouds, and two men were coming there, headfirst like arrows slanting down. And as they came, they sang a sacred song, and the thunder was like drumming. I will sing it for you. The song and drumming were like this: "Behold, a sacred voice is calling you. All over the sky a sacred voice is calling."

I sat there gazing at [the men], and they were coming from the place where the giant lives (north). But when they were very close to me, they wheeled about toward where the sun goes down, and suddenly they were geese. Then they were gone, and the rain came with a big wind and a roaring.

I did not tell this vision to anyone. I liked to think about it, but I was afraid to tell it.

The Sun Dance

About the middle of the Moon of Making Fat (June), the whole village moved a little way up the river to a good place for a Sun Dance. The valley was wide and flat there, and we camped in a great oval with the river flowing through it. In the center, they built the bower of branches in a circle for the dancers, with the opening of it to the east whence comes the light. Scouts were sent out in all directions to guard the sacred place. Sitting Bull, who was the greatest medicine man of the nation at that time, had charge of this dance to purify the people and to give them power and endurance. It was held in the Moon of Fatness because that is the time when

The Sioux followed the movements of the sun and moon to mark the passing seasons.

the sun is highest and the growing power of the world is strongest. I will tell you how it was done.

First a holy man was sent out all alone to find the *waga chun* (rustling tree), a holy tree that should stand in the middle of the dancing circle. Nobody dared follow to see what he did or hear the sacred words he would say there. And, when he had found the right tree, he would tell the people, and they would come there singing, with flowers all over them. Then, when they had gathered about the holy tree, some women who were bearing children would dance around it because the Spirit of the Sun loves all fruit-

fulness. After that, a warrior who had done some very brave deed that summer struck the tree, counting coup on it. And when he had done this, he had to give gifts to those who had least of everything, and the braver he was, the more he gave away.

After this, a band of young maidens came singing, with sharp axes in their hands. [The maidens] had to be so good that nobody there could say anything against them...and it was the duty of anyone who knew anything bad about any of them to tell it right before all the people there and prove it. But if anybody lied, it was very bad for [the liar].

A tribe gathers to watch a young man perform the Sun Dance, an important ceremony among Plains Indians. While dancing, the braves gazed steadily at the sun and blew whistles made of eagle bone.

The maidens chopped the tree down and trimmed its branches off. Then chiefs who were the sons of chiefs carried the sacred tree home, stopping four times on the way, once for each season, giving thanks for each.

Now when the holy tree had been brought home—but was not yet set up in the center of the dancing place—mounted warriors gathered around the oval of the village. At a signal, they all charged inward upon the center where the tree would stand, each trying to be the first to touch the sacred place. And whoever was the first could not be killed in war that year. When they all came together in the middle, it was like a battle, with the ponies rearing and screaming in a big dust and the men shouting and wrestling and trying to throw each other off the horses. After that, there was a big feast and plenty for everybody to eat and a big dance just as though we had won a victory.

The next day, the tree was planted in the center by holy men who sang sacred songs and made sacred vows to the Spirit. And the next morning nursing mothers brought their holy little ones to lay them at the bottom of the tree, so that the sons would be brave men and the daughters the mothers of brave men. The holy men pierced the ears of the little ones, and for each piercing the parents gave away a pony to someone who was in need.

The next day, the dancing began, and those who were going to take part were ready, for they had been fasting and purifying themselves in the sweat lodges and praying. First, their bodies were painted by the holy men. Then each would lie down beneath the tree as though he were dead, and the holy men would cut a place in his back or chest so that a strip of rawhide, fastened to the top of a tree, could be pushed through the flesh and tied. Then the man would get up and dance to the drums, leaning on the rawhide strip as long as he could stand the pain or until the flesh tore loose.

We smaller boys had a good time during the two days of dancing, for we were allowed to do almost anything to tease people, and they had to stand it. We would gather sharp spear grass, and when a man came along without a shirt, we would stick him to see if we could make him cry out, for everybody was supposed to endure everything. Also we made pop-guns out of young ash boughs and shot at the men and women to see if we

In 1876 the U.S. army was attempting to push the Sioux and Cheyenne in the Montana Territory onto reservations. But the Indians fought back. The Battle of Little Bighorn (above) pitted U.S. general George Custer's troops against Sioux and Cheyenne warriors led by Crazy Horse, a Sioux chief. The Indians defeated Custer, killing the general and all his men.

could make them jump. And if they did, everybody laughed at them. The mothers carried water to their holy little ones in bladder bags, and we made little bows and arrows that we could hide under our robes so that we could steal up to the women and shoot holes in the bags. They were supposed to stand anything and not scold us when the water spurted out. We had a good time there.

Right after the Sun Dance was over, some of our scouts came in from the south, and the crier (announcer of important events) went around the circle and said, "The scouts have returned, and they have reported that soldiers are camping up the river. So, young warriors, take courage and get ready to meet them."

At the Rosebud Reservation in South Dakota, Indians line up to receive rations of beef. Although the Sioux fought hard to keep their land, the U.S. government eventually forced them onto reservations.

A Nation in Despair

...It was in the summer of my twentieth year (1883) that I performed the ceremony of the elk. That fall, they say, the last of the bison (buffalo) herds was slaughtered by the Wasichus. I can remember when the bison were so many that they could not be counted, but more and more Wasichus came to kill them until there were only heaps of bones scattered where [the animals] used to be. The Wasichus did not kill them to eat. They killed them for the metal (money) that makes them crazy, and they took only the hides to sell. Sometimes they did not even take the hides, only the tongues, and I have heard that fire-boats came down the Missouri River loaded with dried bison tongues. You can see that the men who did this were crazy. Sometimes they did not even take the tongues. They just killed and killed because they liked to do that. When we hunted bison, we killed only what we needed. And when there was nothing left but heaps of bones, the Wasichus came and gathered up even the bones and sold them.

All our people now were settling down in square gray houses, scattered here and there across this hungry land, and around them the Wasichus had drawn a line to keep them in. The nation's hoop was broken, and there was no center any longer for the flowering tree.[1] The people were in despair. They seemed heavy to me, heavy and dark—so heavy that it seemed they could not be lifted and so dark that they could not be made to see anymore. Hunger was among us often now, for much of what…Washington sent us must have been stolen by Wasichus who were crazy to get money. There were many lies, but we could not eat them. The forked tongue[2] made promises.

I kept on curing the sick for three years more, and many came to me and were made better. But, when I thought of my great vision, which was to save the nation's hoop and make the holy tree to bloom in the center of it, I felt like crying, for the sacred hoop was broken and scattered. The life of the people was in the hoop, and what are many little lives if the life of those lives be gone?…

I looked back on the past and recalled my people's old ways, but they were not living that way any more. They were traveling the black road,[3] everybody for himself and with little rules of his own.…I was in despair, and I even thought that if the Wasichus had a better way, then maybe my people should live that way. I know now that this was foolish, but I was young and in despair.

Glossary

aborigines: The first people known to have lived in a certain place.

birchbark canoe: A low, narrow boat made with a framework of cedar wood covered with birchbark. Indians peeled large sheets of bark from trees, sewed the sheets together and shaped them around the cedar frame. Resins from spruce trees were spread over the birchbark to waterproof the canoe.

counting coup: To touch an enemy in battle without causing injury. Some tribes used a special weapon called a coup stick, but warriors could also touch the enemy with a bow, club, or even a hand. Counting coup was a way of measuring bravery among the Plains warriors.

reservation: An area of land set aside by the U.S. government for Indian people to live on. Some reservations are lands that Indians kept through treaties with the government. Sometimes the government moved the Indians to reservations far from their tribal homelands.

scalp: To cut or tear a part of the scalp and hair from an enemy as a sign of victory in war. An Indian warrior was often judged by the number of scalps collected in battle.

shaman: A traditional tribal spiritual leader. The shaman (or medicine man) keeps tribal history and rituals and attempts to control the supernatural. He uses these powers to cure the sick and to bring forth visions.

travois: A type of all-season sled pulled by dogs or horses. A travois consisted of two poles tied together in the shape of a V. The closed end rested on the animals' shoulders and the open end dragged on the ground. A piece of hide or a plank of wood was placed between the poles to support supplies or people.

warbonnet: A headdress with feathers that each represent different feats in battle.

warpath: The route taken by a party of Indians going to battle.

wigwam: A dwelling shaped like a dome or a cone with a wooden frame overlaid with bark, animal hides, or woven grass mats.

Pronunciation Guide

Anishinabe (an-ish-in-AH-bee)
Cheyenne (shy-AN)
Chippewa (CHIP-uh-wah)
Hidatsa (hih-DAHT-suh)
Kiowa-Apache (KY-uh-wah)-(uh-PA-chee)

Oglala (oh-GLAH-luh)
Ojibway (oh-JIHB-way)
Piegan (PEE-gan)
Sioux (SOO)
Teton (TEE-tahn)

Notes

Chapter 1: Charles A. Eastman

1. The name *Sioux* comes from an Ojibway word for a type of snake. In the Siouan language, the Sioux call themselves *Dakota* (or *Lakota* or *Nakota*, depending on which Siouan dialect is spoken), meaning "allies."
2. *Hakadah*, meaning "the pitiful last," is the name that was given to Eastman at birth. When he was older, he earned the name *Ohiyesa*, which means "winner."
3. "Great Mystery" refers to a supernatural power. Many Indian tribes believed that this power could be gained by certain people or through certain ceremonies. The power might also be centered in some animals or things.

Chapter 2: John Stands In Timber

1. Some use of picture writing existed among the Cheyenne, but it was less developed than among the Kiowa and the Sioux, who had calendar records. Oral traditions were much more important, and accurate transmission of these records was stressed.
2. The ancestral hero Sweet Medicine supposedly passed to the tribe four Sacred Arrows given to him by the Great Spirit. Two of these arrows were for hunting and two were for war. The Sacred Arrows symbolized tribal unity and were kept with other tribal objects.

3. The Cheyenne chiefs' council, or Council of Forty-four, was the most elaborately structured institution of its kind on the Plains. It was composed of four representatives elected from each of the ten tribal bands, with four extra head chiefs held over from the preceding decade's term. The political power of this body began to erode with the intervention of U.S. officials during the middle and late nineteenth century.
4. Also known as the Sweet Medicine Chief.

Chapter 3: Two Leggings
1. The Piegans were a division of the Blackfoot Confederacy, which also included the Blackfoot band, the Blood band, the Gros Ventres, and the Sarcees. These tribes controlled a large section of the northeastern Plains.
2. According to many tribal legends, the Thunderbird caused thunder and lightning.
3. The Crow believed that by fasting they could receive "medicine," or supernatural powers. Medicine dreams—or visions—were regarded as important prophecies and were considered the strongest medicine of all.
4. The length of a vision quest was four days.
5. This prediction was never fulfilled. Two Leggings was never to become a full-fledged chief.
6. A ceremonial lodge in which rocks were heated, and the steam produced was used to purify the body.

Chapter 4: Chief Luther Standing Bear
1. Luther Standing Bear inherited the title of chief from his father.
2. The "Maker of All Things." Also known as the Big Holy.

Chapter 7: Jim Whitewolf
1. Small boys practiced with blunt arrows as a way for them to achieve marksmanship without harming many small animals.
2. "Crazy" meant careless and irresponsible.
3. To hobble a horse is to tie its legs together to keep it from straying.
4. "Opened up" meant the time of extensive white settlement.
5. Instead of aunt, a boy called his father's sister by that very name. The boy's relations with her were restrained and respectful but lacked the element of fear. With a boy's mother's brother's wife, relations were less formal. This aunt by marriage tended to be preferred over the child's father's sister. A boy was on terms of greater familiarity and intimacy with his mother's brother than with any other relative in his parents' generation. This was a close relationship characterized by joking and teasing and by great indulgence on the uncle's part.

Chapter 8: Black Elk
1. The hoop and the tree are sacred symbols that Black Elk received in the "great vision"—the most important vision of his youth. As Black Elk interpreted them, these symbols represented the unity and fruitfulness of the Sioux Nation.
2. One who intends to mislead or deceive.
3. The path of disunity. The departure from traditional customs and beliefs caused by the forced move to reservations.

Sources

Introduction

8   Vine Deloria, Jr. *Custer Died for Your Sins: An Indian Manifesto*, Macmillan, New York, 1969, pp. 239–240.

9   Tom Shakespeare, *The Sky People*, Vantage Press, New York, 1971

Charles A. Eastman

13–14   Charles A. Eastman, *Indian Boyhood*, McClure, Phillips & Company, New York, 1902. Reprinted: Dover Publications, Inc., 1971, New York, pp. 3, 9-10. Used by permission.

14–19   Ibid., pp. 41–49.

John Stands in Timber

23–30   John Stands in Timber and Margot Liberty, *Cheyenne Memories*, with the assistance of Robert M. Utley, Copyright © 1967 by Yale University Press, New Haven and London, pp. 11–13, 27, 42–45. Used by permission.

30–31   Ibid., pp. 40–41.

Two Leggings

35–39   "First War Party," Chapter 3, pp. 11–15 from *Two Leggings: The Making of a Crow Warrior* by Peter Nabokov, Thomas Y. Crowell Company, Inc., New York; Copyright © 1967 by Peter Nabokov. Reprinted with permission of Thomas Y. Crowell Company, Inc.

39–43   Ibid., "The Vision Quest," Chapter 12, pp. 61–65.

Chief Luther Standing Bear

47–58   Chief Luther Standing Bear, *My People, the Sioux*, edited by E. A. Brininstool, with an introduction by William S. Hart, Houghton Mifflin Company, Boston and New York, 1928, pp. 3, 13-27.

58–62   Chief Luther Standing Bear, *Land of the Spotted Eagle*, Houghton Mifflin Company, Boston and New York, 1933, pp. 148–153.

62–69   Ibid., pp. 192–197.

William Whipple Warren

73–77   William W. Warren, *History of the Ojibways, based upon Traditions and Oral Statements*, 1885; New Edition; Ross & Haines, 1957, *History of the Ojibway Nation*, pp. 39–40, 263–266.

Waheenee

81–87   Waheenee, *Waheenee: An Indian Girl's Story*, told by herself to Gilbert L. Wilson, Ph.D., Webb Publishing Company, St. Paul, 1921, pp. 7-13. Reprinted by permission of Webb Publishing Company.

87–91   Ibid., pp. 90–94.

91–97   Ibid., pp. 117–126.

97   Ibid., pp. 175–176.

Jim Whitewolf

101–109 Jim Whitewolf, *Jim Whitewolf: The Life of a Kiowa Apache Indian*, edited and with an introduction and epilogue by Charles S. Brant, Dover Publications, Inc., New York, 1969, pp. 49–53.

Black Elk

113 Black Elk, *Black Elk Speaks: Being the Life Story of a Holy Man of the Oglala Sioux*, as told through John G. Neihardt, 1932. Reprinted: Copyright 1961, University of Nebraska Press, Lincoln, 1961, pp. 9–10. Used by permission.
113–114 Ibid., pp. 18–19.
114–119 Ibid., pp. 95–99.
120–121 Ibid., pp. 217–219.

Index

Photo Acknowledgments

Cover photo: The Philbrook Museum of Art, Tulsa, Oklahoma

Center for Southwest Research, General Library, University of New Mexico, Neg. No. 994-045-0053, p. 1; South Dakota Historical Society-State Archives, pp. 4-5, 12; Painting by Henry F. Farny/William J. Williams Family Collection, pp. 6-7; Robert Czarnomski, pp. 10-11, 32-33; National Archives of Canada, (C-114467-detail), p. 14; © William J. Weber/Visuals Unlimited, pp. 20-21; Archives and Manuscript Division of the Oklahoma Historical Society, pp. 22 (Neg. No. 20485), 29 (Bertoia Collection, Neg. No. 20549.28 R), 30-31; Painting by Dick West/The Philbrook Museum of Art, Tulsa, OK, p. 25; Museum of New Mexico, pp. 26 (Neg. No. 67683/Joseph K. Dixon), 34 (Neg. No. 72679/George W. Griffith), 46 (Neg. No. 91498/Keystone View Co.), 120 (Neg. No. 144750/J. H. Anderson); Painting by Robert Lindneux/Colorado Historical Society, p. 28; Paintings by Karl Bodmer/Independent Picture Service, pp. 37, 56, 60, 85, 92; Rodman Wanamaker/Center for Southwest Research, General Library, University of New Mexico (Neg. No. 994-045-0054), p. 38; Painting by George Catlin/Independent Picture Service, p. 41; South Dakota Department of Tourism, pp. 44-45, 110-111, 115; Minnesota Historical Society, pp. 49 (Seth Eastman), 72 (T.W. Ingersoll); National Anthropological Archives/Smithsonian Institution, pp. 50 (#3700), 106-107 (#77-7721); Fred W. Marvel/Oklahoma Tourism and Recreation Department, pp. 53, 98-99; Wyoming State Museum, pp. 54-55; Denver Public Library, Western History Department, p. 63; Michigan Travel Bureau, p. 64; © David Molchos, pp. 66-67; Kay Shaw, pp. 70-71; Ayer Collection, Newberry Library, p. 74; Painting by Patrick DesJarlait/Photo of painting by John Borge, courtesy of Jim Richards, p. 75; U.S. House of Representatives Art Collection/Architect of the Capitol, p. 76; North Dakota Department of Tourism, pp. 78-79; Montana State University-Billings, pp. 80, 84; James J. Hill Collection, p. 83; American Museum of Natural History/Department of Library Services, p. 86 (Neg. No. 2A13767), 112 (Neg. No. 19855), 116-117 (painting by Short Bull/Neg. No. 326847); Culver Pictures, p. 89; Painting by George Catlin/National Museum of American Art, Washington, D.C./Art Resource, NY, pp. 90-91 (detail); Harold Case Collection/State Historical Society of North Dakota, p. 95; Arizona Historical Society/Tuscon (photo #60405) p. 100; Research Division, Arizona Department of Library, Archives, and Public Records, Phoenix, p. 103; Western History Collections, University of Oklahoma, p. 104; American Heritage Center, University of Wyoming, p. 108; Painting by Kicking Bear/The Southwest Museum, Los Angeles, Photo #(CT.1), p. 119; J. Wylder/Montana Travel, p. 123